I0160908

The
Kiki Chronicles:

An
Equispecial Journey

By

Kiki Osbourne

Illustrated by
Kiki Osbourne

© 2003 by Kiki Osbourne. All rights reserved.

No part of this book may be reproduced,
stored in a retrieval system, or transmitted by any
means, electronic, mechanical, photocopying,
recording, or otherwise, without written permission
from the author.

ISBN: 978-0-9766965-3-7

Library of Congress Control Number: 2003093250

This book is printed on acid free paper.

Printed in the United States of America

"In the Eye of the Horse

The Magic Resides"

For all horses, who are keepers of the magic,
Especially for Cactus, who started the magic…
And, for Dappir, where it still resides…

Contents

Forwards

Early Years With Kiki...

I am pleased to write an introduction to this creative, wonderful book. Kiki was a young student of mine, and I have had the fun, and honor, of guiding her through the early years of learning the 'ropes', as well as through her first eventing competitions.

As I recall my years with Kiki, what stands out the most about this remarkable young woman is her approach to the world of equestrian sport. She was, as a student, always eager, curious, brave, and open-minded about what she was learning, or being asked to do – which made her a true joy to teach and mentor along the way. Kiki simply loved to learn new things.

And, as this book shows, Kiki was not content to simply educate herself. Through her articles, she reached out to others, wanting to share what knowledge she gained so that everyone could enjoy the horses and the learning process as she did.

Reading through this collection of stories, so many memories come back...Kiki entering her very first mini-event, and winning it despite learning the rules literally as she went along! Early lessons – as she struggled to figure out how to canter while riding in a ring that required her and Cactus to dodge trees and stumps as they went!

There are also many firsts I have shared with Kiki: her first serious competitions, her first lessons as an instructor, her first horses in training, and her first professional trainer job. Through it all, Kiki always stayed being Kiki – she asked for advice when needed, figured things out on her own when she could, experimented with what worked and what didn't, and kept asking questions – usually beginning with "why?" And she ALWAYS gave back. After accomplishing her United States Pony Club A rating, a difficult and admirable achievement, Kiki began helping other pony clubbers, teaching them both mounted and unmounted horsemanship skills.

As her reputation grew, it was notable that her ego did not. Kiki still today can always be counted on to take the modest path, and downplay her successes, without minimizing herself in the process. As I watch Kiki continue to develop as a horse professional and as a person, I am so proud of her, at whom she has become, and where she is going.

As you read through these pages, you will be able to experience "my Kiki," and smile at the eager young rider who so openly and honestly shared her insights, triumphs and tribulations on her way to a horse career. So sit back, enjoy yourself, and take a trip back with me down memory lane.

Kathy Kelly, PhD

Later Years With Kiki...

Ten years ago my best friend Kathy Kelly introduced me to a young girl she had been helping. She said she was special. After meeting her, with some skepticism, and making fun of her unusual name – my relationship with Kiki began.

A very special relationship it was, and still is. Kiki was a working student for me for several years and was a true joy to have around. She was the most level-headed teenager I have ever had the pleasure of being around. No matter the work, the stress, the pressure, the joy, and the pain that goes with the horse business – I could always count on Kiki just hanging in the boat.

Kiki is also a very talented rider (as well as many other things) which was just icing on the cake. I greatly enjoyed having her in my life and going from her mentor to her friend (I hope!!).

Cathy Jones Forsberg, Trainer

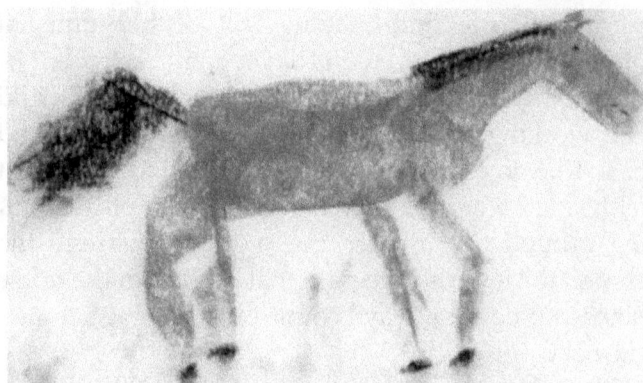

Introduction

Choosing To Live Your Life
On Four Legs!

To a large extent, life is about your ability to make the best choices you can make. Now you also should understand that the choices you make today will have lots to do with the possibilities you have to choose from tomorrow, next week, next month, next year…really, the rest of your life.

There is a world full of possibilities out there…and one of the first stories I ever remember my dad telling me was the one about "the one-legged stool that fell over." What he meant was that in order to become a well rounded interesting human being, I needed to have more than one focus in my life. Otherwise, like the one-legged stool, I would fall over too.

I Simply Loved Horses…

In my own case, I knew at a very early age that I loved everything about horses. I liked riding them. I liked feeding them. I liked grooming them. I liked competing them. And my parents allowed me to indulge myself in my four-legged passion, as long as I took care of things in school and I had "more than one leg on my stool." Pony Club and 4H allowed me to "add a couple of legs." In addition to the horse project in 4H, I liked art and photography as a hobby and I incorporated them into my 4H projects.

Along the road, I added music to my life. I joined the Glen Ellyn Children's Chorus. I was given an opportunity to sing with a remarkable group, many of whom became part of my circle of friends. We performed around the U.S., Canada and Europe.

My mom and dad used to say that they knew they could always find me at one of three places: School, Chorus, or the Barn. (The three main legs of my "stool.") But I always knew that the equestrian leg was where my heart was.

And I Also Had To Help Pay For The Horse...

There was one other part of the deal I need to tell you about. My parents wanted me to do something to help pay for my horse activities, because as my dad always reminded me, "horses aren't cheap." And the thing I chose to do to make money was to write a monthly horse column for kids. I called it *Equispecial: A Horse Column For Kids.* I charged $25 per column and I wrote it for five consecutive years...60 columns. It was carried in several different equine publications. This book is a collection of the best of those columns that I wrote over a decade ago in order to earn money to help pay for my equine activities.

Now as you begin to read, just think of yourself as riding alongside, a real live partner in the adventures of a young horse person who wanted more than anything to live her entire life on four graceful legs, with a mane and tail flying in the wind. That was me, does it sound like you too? Now, here's what you can look forward to learning about in the following chapters.

Responsibility: caring for a horse is a big job. *Decision-making*: how to choose your four legged friend. *Friendship*: the unbelievable feeling you get just walking into a barn to greet your new "friend," or those people who are always there. *Work ethic*: The work is never done when you are in the horse world. *Courage*: accomplishing a feat you thought you would never be able to do. *Teamwork*: competing together at Pony Club rallies, all for the team. *Knowledge*: Learning how to care for another living being.

These and much more, are all yours if you open your soul to the world of the horse, and absorb all that you can, just because you are lucky enough to be there, like I was.

And when you're done reading my story, I suggest that you think about the choices you have to make now, and how they will relate to the possibilities that you will have to choose from in the future. Whether or not you love horses the way that I did, if you follow your heart, the choices you make will be clear and focused on moving you day by day into the barn, into the stall, into the saddle, into the arena, over the jumps, and into a life that is chuck full of four legged fun and adventure no matter where your dreams take you. Now, check out the following chapters and we'll catch up again at the end of the book.

Living my life on four legs

The First Year

All your pony
asks is to be

kept clean, dry,

fed, watered, warm,

~ and loved

1

The ABCs of Grooming

Have you ever wondered why you have to use a curry comb, or a hard brush, or a hoof pick on your horse? Well, if you are wondering what each of the brushes do, I'll tell you.

The first brush to use on your horse or your pony should be the curry comb. You use the curry comb by rubbing hard in a circular manner. The curry comb, if used this way, loosens dirt, dried mud, or extra hair on your horse.

The next brush you should use is the hard-bristled brush. To correctly use the hard-bristled brush, you should work in short, wispy strokes. This technique takes all the loose hair, dirt and dried mud off your horse.

The body brush or soft-bristled brush should be used after the hard-bristled brush. The soft brush is used just like the hard brush, and it will take off the rest of the little dirt particles that are left by the hard brush. This brush is also to be used on the face of your horse. It should be soft enough so it does not irritate the eyes or any other part of the face.

To pick the horse's hooves, you need a hoof pick. To pick a hoof, you slide two fingers down along both sides of the tendon. The horse's natural response will be to pick up his hoof. Grab the hoof so you have good control over it. Next, find the frog (the v-shaped part on the bottom of the horse's foot), put the pick underneath it, then stroke hard until all the mud is out. It is important to pick your horse's hooves, because if he picks up a stone and you don't get it out soon afterward, he could develop a lameness.

If your horse has rolled or wandered into some brush and messed up his mane, you surely need a mane-and-tail comb. A mane-and-tail comb is very simple to use. Just pretend that the mane or the tail is your own hair and brush until all the knots are out.

Two extra brushes you might need are the shedding blade and sweat scraper. The shedding blade is very useful when your horse is shedding. It takes away all of the excess hair that he sheds. All you have to do to use this brush is to make long, even strokes down your horse's body, and he will look nice and shiny.

One last brush to keep handy is the sweat scraper. This is useful when your horse gets sweaty or gets a bath and is wet. You use this brush the way you use the shedding blade, and it will take most of the water off your horse.

There you have it, the seven brushes you should always have in your brush box. They are: the curry comb, the hard-bristled brush, the body brush, the hoof-pick, the mane-and-tail comb, the shedding blade and the sweat scraper. Keep in mind, your horse is depending on YOU to keep him clean. Don't let him down.

Kiki Osbourne

At the Fun Day
Honey and Kate in poodle skirts
win the costume class

2

Equispecial Fun Day

Some people might think that showing their horse is the only reason to own a horse. But I certainly don't think that! I enjoy riding my horse just for the fun of it. I suggest all horse owners should take time out to have a little fun with their four-legged friends.

In late October, the barn where I board my horses sponsored a fun day. This was simply a day where people and their horses could have fun together. All the friends of the stable were invited. Some people cared so much about having "fun" with their horses that they drove a full hour to attend this get-together.

Since it was so close to Halloween, we dressed up our horses in Halloween costumes. I dressed up my horse as a clown; my brother dressed his as Bambi. Among the other entries were an Indian pony, a '50's horse, and even a psychedelic horse. Ribbons were then awarded for the best-dressed horses.

After the costume class, we played a series of games that are not generally associated with horses. These were "Boot Race," "Egg and Spoon," "Water

Race," "Chug-a-lug Race," "Dizzy Cowboy," "Simon Says," "Balloon Toss," "Trail Class," "Ride-a-Buck," and "Bribe Your Horse."

Of course, we liked some of these games more than others. My brother liked "Simon Says" the best. This was the longest of all the games, so BEWARE if you decide to try it. To play, you must listen very closely to the commands made by the announcer (it also helps if your HORSE understands English!), and make sure you don't make a move without those magic words, "Simon Says." For example, if the announcer says, "trot," do not trot until she says, "Simon says, trot." If you make a wrong move, you are eliminated from the group. We played for a very long time because we had some people who were very good at this!.

My personal favorite was the water race. While on horseback, we each held a cup of water filled to the brim. You had to hold the cup in one hand at a walk, trot and canter. Afterwards, someone measured the amount of water that was left in each cup. I had the most water left in my cup, and won first place — which is why this was my favorite!

We finished the day with a pot-luck dinner and a pinata. Everyone enjoyed the entire day, and I hope it will become an annual activity for my brother and me.

Some of you riders who take riding so seriously should really think of having a little fun with your four-legged friend.

Why not suggest this idea of holding a fun day at YOUR barn? You'll love it!

Huntseat Riders
Honey and Kate, Brittany and me, Rose and Amy

3

Equispecial Riding Styles Part 1, Huntseat

When I took my first lesson, I thought that horseback riding was just a matter of staying upright on the horse's back. I didn't realize that there are many styles of riding.

The four that I am most familiar with are Huntseat, Saddleseat, Dressage and Western. This article about Huntseat is the first in a four part series which talks about these four styles of riding.

Huntseat developed in England where fox hunting is a popular sport. I learned that huntseat is the most relaxed form of English style riding. It is generally not as stiff as saddle seat or as relaxed as western. It is sort of "in-between."

Often people think that all hunters are thoroughbreds, but there are many different breeds used as hunters. Some of these include Arabians, Quarter Horses, Warmbloods, and sometimes even Saddlebreds! Shetland, Welsh Mountain, and New

Forest ponies are occasionally used as hunter-jumpers, too.

Once you have chosen your horse or pony, you need to think about the tack. There are several types of saddles that work well for huntseat riding. These range from close contact, to padded kneel roll saddles. Depending on your horses, use a thick or thin pad to protect his spine. Use a full bridle. An eggbut snaffle is the most common hunter practice bit.

In shows you might prefer to use a full check cheek bit or a full cheek twisted wire snaffle, just for extra control. Don't use the wire twisted snaffle bit unless absolutely necessary — you wouldn't want your horse to develop a hard mouth! Something that surprised me was that the fatter bit, which looks so big and uncomfortable, is actually the gentlest one for my horse.

One last item: If you start jumping seriously, you might want to buy galloping boots to protect your horse's ankles and cannon bones (the largest bone in the horse's lower leg) in case he knocks a fence down.

Once you are up, you need to know that your position in huntseat riding is very important whether on the flat or jumping. On the flat, your eyes should be looking in the direction that you are moving. Your hands should be held steady at a 45 degree angle. The finger and thumb should be securely tightened around the reins and placed right above your horse's withers. Your leg should be right under your shoulder and a little behind the girth. Your heel should be down and relaxed. The ball of your foot should be right at the end of the stirrup. A flat back is also required for good hunt seat riding.

Once you have mastered the flat, you are ready to start jumping. Shortening your stirrups is good to help your balance. To prepare to jump, lean forward in the saddle, bend your knees onto the knee rolls and have your heels as far down as possible. This is known as a "two-point". Your eyes are always either looking at the obstacle or straight ahead. You should always look at the obstacle when heading towards the jump. When you jump the obstacle, look straight ahead or at the next obstacle.

To complete the picture, there are even different types of clothing worn depending upon the type of riding you choose. At a 4-H clinic, I learned that huntseat rider apparel is supposed to fit all types of weather. Knee boots are for keeping you lower legs warm and protected from tree branches on the hunt course. Breeches are used to cover the upper leg.

The collar on the hunt blouse is used to keep your neck warm, and the pin on the collar is for good luck. I used to use an old initial pin of my Mom's, but for Christmas I got a beautiful gold horse-shoe/horse head pin. I'm sure that it will be my good luck charm for this year's show season, and I need all the luck I can get! Last of all is the helmet, which is used to protect your head in case of a fall.

Huntseat is just one of the styles that I have tried. I suggest that if you haven't ridden huntseat, give it a try. Maybe it will be your cup of tea!

Equispecial
Kid's Corner
by Kendra Gail Osbourne

 Equi Special For Kids!
BY KENDRA OSBOURNE

Every stable has its own speci~
vantages and disadvanta~
ple, the place wh~
Kingswa~ ~

MidWest Equine Marke~

Page 8

EQUISPECIAL
A Horse Column
For Kids... By Kids!

Saddleseat Riding

~
d
ar
fli
kne
O.
part
large
finishe
nounce
weeken
this!
We ari
saw in hai
was hard t
of brush an
of worker~

Yet another style of English riding, in
~bnt seat and dressage is
~~~ is a

bred, Rose, using several interesti~
techniques. Stretchers, trubber band li~
ropes that tie around the horses hoov~
~re used to strengthen the muscles
~~ing, chains aro~

4

Equispecial Riding Styles Part 2, Saddleseat

Yet another style of English riding, in addition to hunt seat and dressage is saddleseat. Generally, saddleseat is a very formal style of riding. When I first started taking lessons, I was riding saddleseat and didn't even realize that there was any other style.

Recently I had a conversation with Liz Rice of Shilke Farms, Yorkville, IL, and a local expert in saddleseat riding. I discovered a number of interesting things about this unique style of riding. To begin with, I learned that Saddlebreds, Morgans, and Arabians are the most common breeds of horses used in saddleseat riding. The primary reason for this is because of their unique head carriage.

Saddlebreds are either three gaited or five gaited. The three gaited horses walk, trot and canter. These horses have more up and down motion in their strides and the five gaited horses have more forward motion. In addition to walk, trot, and canter, they have two man-made gaits that only Saddlebreds can learn: the slow gait and the rack. These particular gaits are four beat gaits where only one hoof at a time touches the ground. Just about every Saddlebred can be trained to slow gait and to rack.

My friend Amy trained her Saddlebred, Rose, using several interesting techniques. Stretchers (rubber band like ropes that tie around the horses hooves) were used to strengthen the muscles in her legs. Action chains, chains around her feet that make clinking noises when she moved, were put around her hooves to make her pick up her feet, although a lot of this movement comes naturally to the Saddlebred. She also used a running martingale, a piece of leather attached to the bridle and girth, to make sure that her head was up and tucked.

The rider carries himself as tall and as thin as possible. The riders ride high handed because their horses have very long necks. If3 their hands were held low, the horse could look like a giraffe!

Saddleseat riding has little lower leg contact. To control the horse, you usually use the upper leg from the knee to the thigh. If you are watching someone ride saddleseat, you should be able to imagine a line connecting the rider's ear, shoulder, hip, knee, and heel.

The tack used for saddleseat riding is a cutback saddle. The cutback is an English style saddle without a pommel. The saddleseat rider uses a double bridle. The double bridle consists of two bits, a snaffle and a curb. The snaffle is to control your horse, and the curb is to make the horse tuck his head. This type of bridle also has two reins.

So why do people ride saddleseat? I asked Liz. She said "It's not so much riding saddle seat, it's the American Saddlebred. It is a thrilling breed to ride! The American Saddlebreds are incredibly powerful and smooth!" After talking with her I discovered that Liz was twice World Champion and once a Reserve World Champ as well.

You may be wondering what these riders wear. For every day riding they wear riding jodhpurs and short boots. The reason for wearing short boots is because of the little lower leg contact. For showing before 6 p.m., they wear "saddlesuits." These suits resemble a men's business suit because years ago men rode horses straddle and women rode side-saddle. Through the years the formal suit stuck. I found it interesting that if they show after 6 p.m., riders can be very formal and wear tuxedos.

All in all, saddleseat is a sophisticated type of riding. The horse moves beautifully, and it is a very athletic event.

Kiki Osbourne

"Dressage"

5

Equispecial Riding Styles Part 3, Dressage

Dressage is a type of riding that many kids aren't exposed to. This is probably true because their parents don't want to pay $750 for a jacket and $500 for a top hat. Nonetheless, from the little exposure that I've had, dressage has impressed me as a fascinating style of riding.

Describing dressage is not easy. I would say that it comes closer to a "dancing horse" than anything else I can think of. I noticed that the dressage horse has a fluid, stretched, but extremely well controlled gait. He also has a rounded neck, and his head is tucked down, which makes him look quite fashionable with his braided mane. I discovered later that the rider is the real control element, and that the three positions of dressage riding play a large role in his ability to control the horse.

Dressage also takes place in a different kind of ring. There are no high fences, but instead the ring is surrounded by letters toward which the horse's actions are directed. This is probably the main reason why dressage competition is uncommon in most horse shows today.

I learned from my dressage teacher, Therese Solomon that my thoroughbred, Brittany, would work out great as a dressage horse. Brittany has a well balanced body and good conformation (how a horse is "put together" or "built"). There are many different breeds of horses used in dressage, but the most popular, from what I've seen, is the Warmblood.

For beginning dressage I've learned that you don't need all of the formal dressage tack. At first I thought there was no way that I could ride dressage with my huntseat tack, but Therese told me I didn't need all the extras if I was just a beginner.

In my first dressage lesson I learned that there are three leg positions. The first one is used to maintain a straight line and your leg should be right at the girth. The second is used to hold the horse in place and for bending your horse. In this position your leg should be about two to four inches behind the girth. The third position is used to ask for canter transitions. In this position your leg is placed about four to six inches behind the girth. The positions the rider and the types of control go hand in hand.

I first saw dressage in the 1984 Olympics, before I ever started to ride regularly, and even then I was awed by the horses' movements. Since then, I've still just seen dressage on television, so I am very excited that I will be seeing some dressage classes "live" at the Aux Sable horse show on April 30. This will also be the first time I have ever seen dressage performed by people I know.

Even with the few classes I've taken, I've found dressage to be both fun and interesting. Dressage, though, like everything else, takes a lot of concentration and practice if you want to be good.

If you haven't tried dressage yet, consider taking at least one lesson just to get a feel for it, and, by the time you reach the high level of competition, your parents will have had plenty of time to save their money for that official outfit!!

"Western Gear"

6

Equispecial Riding Styles Part 4, Western

Yeeeeee-ha! Ride 'em Cowboy! That's what I used to think of whenever anyone mentioned Western riding to me. Over the past few years I learned that there are not only several types of English riding, but also different types of Western riding. This will be the last article dealing with different riding styles, and I decided to talk to Heidi Henry, my instructor, about this particular style.

I'll bet that most of you have begged your parents to take you horseback riding and have convinced them to rent a horse for a trail ride that usually lasts an hour. You would most likely be riding "Western," using a Western saddle. This type of saddle has a "horn" that seems to be a security blanket for the inexperienced rider because there is something to hang on to! The experienced rider only holds on to the reins, not his saddle.

23

Although I ride mostly English, I have had a chance to ride Western after we got our quarter horse, Cactus. A Western saddle just happened to come with him! I also have had an opportunity this year to show him Western, and I found out that this type of riding is a lot harder that I thought. The first two types of Western riding that Heidi and I talked about are the types I have worked with most. The last two I have had less experience with, but I have played games on horseback at our 4-H clinic and Fun Day at our barn.

Anyway, to begin with, Heidi and I talked about Western pleasure. In Western pleasure shows, the judge is evaluating the horse and how it moves. The pleasure horse should move slowly and be a pleasure to ride. My mom always tells me to look "pleasurable" when I ride in a Western pleasure class. Almost any breed of horse can be used as a Western pleasure horse, although the quarter horse is the most popular.

In Western horsemanship, you are judged on how you handle your horse. Therefore you can hold your reins shorter and your horse can have a faster pace than in Western pleasure. In this case, you must show off your skills.

Another kind is just called Western riding. This includes reining. Western riding is patterned riding consisting of low jumps and orange cone exercises like weaving in and out at the canter, and changing leads. Western riding is judged on how fast and how well the pattern is executed. For this sport you would want an energetic horse.

Lastly, we get to the fun stuff—the "ya-hoo"—Western gaming. This includes barrel races, pole bending, key hole race and the plug race. These are all judged on speed. You'll want a very spirited horse for this, too!

Just as in any of the other types of riding I talked about previously, there is a certain type of clothing that is appropriate for Western riding. Jeans, Western boots, and a cowboy shirt and hat are the basics. I found that most people who "show" Western also wear chaps and can get pretty fancy in matching colors!

One thing that stands out to me is the FANCY tack that is sometimes used in Western riding. Silver and studs seem to be very popular, and make a very ATTRACTIVE package on a horse. A breast plate gives the horse a very finished look. Most of the really serious riders match tack with their outfits, and the results are quite stunning. If you have never seen Western riding in shows, why not give it a "look-see"—it could be quite entertaining, not to mention exciting!

I hope that I have been able to tell you some new things about ALL of the various types of riding-Hunt Seat, Dressage, Saddleseat, and Western—in these past four articles. It has been fun for me to try all of them and then be able to let you know something about each of them. It seems that even with horses, there is something for everyone. I like new challenges and I can guarantee that you will never be bored when you are involved in the world of horses! Yeeeee-Ha!

Me an' my Breyer herd

7

Breyers, Breyers, Breyers

Boy, I think I'm a lucky girl to be able to have 60 horses of my very own. I love my horses for a lot of reasons. These horses are powerful, graceful and beautiful. Furthermore, I don't have to groom them or muck out their stalls, and they don't cost anything to feed or to keep up! That's my kind of horse! They're called Breyer horse MODELS.

I recently called Ms. Arlene Bentley to find out more about Breyer horses. She is the President of Bentley Sales Co., Des Plaines, Ill., a local Breyer distributor. I found out that Breyers are copied from pictures and made to look like real horses as much as possible. Believe me, they do! Breyers are either modeled after a famous horse, or a certain breed of horse. In the past 20 years, more than 100 different models have been introduced.

Breyers were first introduced in the mid-fifties and are now distributed all over the world. Over the years, collectors began to organize Breyer model horse shows. I'll bet you are wondering how you can have a horse show with just model horses. Right?

I wanted to know, too, so I asked Ms. Bentley about it. She told me that model horse shows try to resemble a real horse show as much as possible. Breyer collectors bring their models to a scheduled horse show and enter in classes that are appropriate for a particular breed of horse. For instance, a thoroughbred would be in a hunter class.

Some people even repaint or remold their horses. When a horse is remolded, it is made to look as if it is approaching a jump, or, perhaps, performing a different gait. From what I've heard, model horse shows are a lot of fun, and I would really like to try to enter one sometime.

All my friends seem to wonder how I got started collecting Breyers. Well, a couple of years ago my mom brought out a horse collection that she had when she was my age. Most of them were ceramic, so she only let me keep the plastic models in my room. These happened to include a 1964 Breyer mare and foal. I had no ideal that they were Breyers until my Grandma bought me three more of them.

Little did I know I was starting my collection four years ago. I was captivated at the sight of the beautiful models. Later, I noticed a little Breyer symbol on the inside of one of their hind legs. That's how I found out I had these two...no, these five Breyers. From there on out, I started buying and receiving as gifts more and more Breyers. Now I have 60!!!

There are so many things you can do with Breyers besides leaving them on your shelf. My friends and I play with my Breyers all the time, we pretend we own a stable or ranch, or we have our own horse show! Several weeks ago I was in a 4H mini fair and showed a representation of my collection of Breyers. I took these horses, put tack (general term for equipment used for riding a horse) and riders on them, put a riding ring around them, and labeled it. "A Typical Show Scene." And, guess what? For that effort I won a championship ribbon!

Where can you find these wonderful horses that require little upkeep and provide years of enjoyment? Usually I can find Breyers at local toy, gift, and card shops. Sometimes I order from horsey catalogs. But, since I discovered this distributor nearby, I now have a local source that carries the complete Breyer line, and some discontinued models as well.

If your parents aren't ready to buy you that horse you've been dreaming of, I think that the next best thing is having a Breyer horse collection.

We decorated our stalls

8

Pajama Party With Your Horse!

Looking for a good time? Want to get to know your horse better? Then come to a week-end horse clinic! That's what I did a few weeks ago, with my 4-H group and my horse, Cactus. Not only did we work on riding and showmanship, but we also spent time with our horses AROUND THE CLOCK!

At the clinic I learned ways to perfect my English and Western riding skills. First, a professional instructor came and gave us some special tips on hunt seat riding. Most of the time we worked on transitions. Transitions are agents of change, and in this case we were changing from walking to trotting or cantering. We practiced walking 15 steps and then trotting 10 steps. Then we walked 15 strides and cantered 10 strides. I found this to be very helpful because in horse shows you are judged on how well you can get your horse to change from one gait to the next.

After working on transitions we worked on balance for a while by dropping our stirrups. This technique really forces you to concentrate on your position in the saddle and it also works some muscles that you may have never worked before. Even though it was not the most exciting part of the clinic. I know that it really helped me (and my muscles!) a lot.

After switching to Western, we worked a lot on jogging and especially on getting our heels down. I also learned a lot about cantering, or loping, as they call it in Western riding circles. The girl teaching the class told us to pull back while squeezing gently to get our horses to slow down properly. Sometimes you are simply reminded of things that you already know, but that still helps.

After we worked all day sharpening our riding skills, our reward was Game Night. ALL RIGHT! First we played "Musical Sacks," which is a lot like the old favorite, "Musical Chairs." In this game you mount your horse and walk him around the sacks until the music stops. Them you jump off your horse and stand on a sack. If you can't find a sack, you are eliminated.

Next, we played "Egg and Spoon." In "Egg and Spoon," each participant gets an egg to balance on a spoon. Then you walk, trot, and canter while trying to keep the egg on the spoon. When your egg drops, you are eliminated from the competition. When there are six participants left, they start determining places through the process of elimination. I kept my egg on the spoon the longest so I won first place. WHAT FUN!

Finally, we did the "Water Race." We were given a full glass of water and again had to walk, trot, and canter with it in one hand. Whoever finishes with the most water in his glass, wins. This game, along with "Egg & Spoon," requires some smooooth riding, and having a smooooth horse doesn't hurt either! Cactus and I hit some bumps and only got a second in this one.

After the games we got ready for bed. Did you ever sleep in a stall before? Well, that's where you sleep at this horse clinic! My friends (Sarah, Kathy, and Amy) and I were lucky, though. We got to sleep on an air mattress because Amy's dad didn't want us to sleep on cold gravel. At least 10,000 covers were piled on top of us. We talked long into the night about how we did in our clinic. Kathy was being a nut by singing weirdly.

You really get to know your horse by spending the night with him. For instance, all night the horses were chewing in their stalls. That annoyed me! Some of the boards in the stall were rotten and falling apart. But we (or the horses) didn't mind. The stalls were only about 50 yards from the train tracks, and every time a train came by, Sarah and I woke up. Every so often I would wake up to check on Cactus. When I went to his stall he kept whinnying at me. I think he likes me! I hope he didn't get the idea that I would be spending every night with him.

On Sunday morning the 4-H held a mock horse show, so we could show off our newly-learned skills. There were English, Western, and Halter classes, but I participated in English and Western classes only.

Because this was a mock horse show, only "Ratings Ribbons" were given out. This was good, because everyone got a ribbon, no matter what.

After the show we packed up and headed home. This year I learned a lot about riding and my horse, and I had fun in the process. I can't wait until next year, or the next clinic!!

9

Touring The Tack

Before I ever walked in, the aroma of new leather literally poured through the cracks in the front door out onto the sidewalk. Once in, I saw everything I ever could have wanted for my horses. A nice tack shop is truly a horse owner/lover's paradise. From apple treats to vitamins...from apparel to Breyer horses to mugs...anything for and about horses...you can find it at a tack shop. Let's explore!

One of the first things you'll notice is the piles and piles of saddles. That is the place I usually like to start. When I was buying my first saddle I was amazed at this array...I thought that you bought either an English or Western saddle...period. Wrong! You can find hundreds of styles and brands of both English and Western, depending upon your style of riding—pleasure, show, jumping, dressage, barrel racing, etc. Oh, check out the prices and you will also see a wide range as well, from $100 to $5,000. My favorite saddle (and I hope to get one for Christmas—hint, hint, mom, if you're reading this) is the Steuben close contact.

Of course, if you are buying a saddle you probably are looking for a bridle (the equipment that goes on the horse's head and has a bit attached), as well, and tack shops seem to carry thousands of bridles. There are several different varieties of bridles. Some of them have braided browbands and nosebands. Some just have plain strips of leather. These are not as fancy, but are still functional. Western bridles range from plain old leather bridles to very fancy ones that have silver rhinestones to match a specific saddle. Bits (the metal piece that goes in the horse's mouth) are abundant. Some tack shops have a full wall devoted to bits alone, in all shapes and sizes! I never knew that horses might prefer one bit over another, or that I needed more than one bit. If you can't find the right bit for your horse, you have a mighty picky animal!

No excuses for not having a well groomed horse, because if you head over to the brush bins, you can find everything you need to have yourself the handsomest horse in town. Choosing these grooming tools can be fun! There are colorful hoof picks and currycombs. I love looking at all this paraphernalia when I buy brushes for my horses. I buy the rainbow colored ones because that seems to be what my horses prefer. (Really, they told me!)

I also like to look at the halters ("head collar" that goes over a horse's nose and head, used to lead a horse) and lead lines. Variety is also the name of the game here. They have leather halters and nylon halters. Some even have hearts stenciled on them. Brittany (one of my horses) wants me to buy her a pink one with hearts.

Blankets and more blankets, coolers, saddle pads, leg wraps, mane tamers, and anything else you want to put on your horse can be found in the tack shop as well. You can color-coordinate your horse in just about anything — designer clothes for horses???

Speaking of designer clothes...when you are tired of getting just about EVERYTHING for your spoiled horse, you can turn to the racks and racks of riding clothes for YOURSELF! I just love pawing through all the different types of clothes. They carry all kinds of English clothes like breeches, shirts, hunt coats, and boots. For Western riders, there are colorful shirts, jeans, vests, and ties of all colors.

Even if you don't own a horse you can't resist the gift section of the tack shop. Some of my friends buy horse magazines so they can learn more about horses. Others love the Breyer horse section and add to their Breyer collections. They also have many mugs and other ceramic articles with horses on them. You can buy ash trays with hunt scenes or even license plates with barrel racers on them.

Where can you go to experience this horse shopper's paradise? There are probably several located in your area...check the yellow pages under "Riding Apparel or Equipment." I have been able to talk my mom into visiting several shops in our area, all the way from St. Charles to Palatine.

As you can probably tell, I love to go to the tack shop. The next time you "need" to go to one, check out everything you can, but be prepared to spend some time! It is really great fun, and your horse will thank you for it!

My friend Gus and Me

10

Friends: That Unique Relationship Between Horse And Rider

I have a friend named Kate, and Kate has a friend named Honey. But Kate is a teenaged girl, and Honey is Kate's horse. Several weeks ago Kate asked me if I would give Honey a workout, since she hadn't been out to the stable in over a week. I said, "Sure," thinking to myself, "Boy, what fun this will be!"

Mom took me out to the barn. When we got there, I saddled up Honey and took her out into the arena. I jumped on and asked Honey to walk and to trot. She did it perfectly. But, when I asked her to canter, she kept taking the wrong lead, throwing her head up, and going wild. I got her calmed down, and then tried her over a few fences. But again she bucked, threw her head and tried to pull the reins out of my hands.

Just then it occurred to me. Honey always does everything that Kate asks her to do without any problem. It was right then that I realized that the relationship between a horse and his "regular rider" is very special.

For example, my horse Brittany will only let me and a couple of other people put on her blanket. Last year, a worker at the barn tried unsuccessfully to put Brittany's blanket on her. Brittany spun around, kicked, and would not give the worker a chance to get it on. Then I went in and Brit stood perfectly still while I put on the blanket. Brittany knows me and is used to me, so we work well together.

Every time I walk by Cactus, one of my other horses, he paces back and forth and whinnies. My newest horse, Outryder, doesn't quite know me yet, so she just looks up when I pass by. But, I don't take it personally; after all, with horses, just like humans, it takes time to get to know someone.

My friend Shannon has been riding horses longer than any teenager I know (since age 3, I'm told). Shannon has a number of ponies, but she has one, Brownie, that she is especially fond of. When Shannon sits on Brownie's neck and says, "Up," Brownie picks up his head, sliding Shannon back into the saddle. Another thing Shannon can do with Brownie is ski from his tail. I doubt if anyone else could get away with these things, but Brownie loves Shannon just as much as Shannon loves him, so he plays along.

One of my favorite horses at our barn is named Magnetic, and he's owned by another friend of mine named Marcy. "Maggie" is a white and gray Arabian that could jump a house if Marcy asked him to. Marcy has owned Maggie for seven years and, after she rides him, Marcy always pulls off the saddle and bridle in the ring. Magnetic, without a halter or a lead rope, follows Marcy to the crossties.

When Magnetic is in the pasture and sees Marcy, he comes running to her. At shows, when Marcy sits down to rest, Maggie lays his head on her shoulder and falls asleep. At the end of the day, Marcy usually gives Maggie a kiss on the nose. But, if Marcy forgets, Maggie pounds the stall door with his hoof until Marcy comes back and gives him his kiss.

People can say what they want about man's best friend (a dog, right?), but for my money, the relationship between a horse and his rider is hard to beat. If you have an equine friend that you are close to, write and tell me about it.

Honey and her friend Kate

The Second Year

Mom, Cactus and I look over the day's mail

11

Equispecial Mailbag I

Since I've been writing my column, I have received many letters asking me questions about horses and my writing. I'd like to take time to answer some of them this month.

Q. *I'm a beginning rider who has learned a lot by reading your column. I'm trying to talk my parents into buying a horse, but they say it is too expensive. Can you help?*

A. Sometimes, before you invest money into a horse of your own, it is a good idea to "share board" — that is, pay half board on someone else's horse, so you can see how much work is involved in having your own horse. It will also give your parents an idea of the costs involved when they talk with the horse's owner. I'm afraid I can't tell you that it isn't expensive, because it is. But...you'll never really know until you give it a try.

Another friend writes...

Kiki Osbourne

Q. How much time do you spend with your horses every week? I want a horse of my own, but I am afraid I won't have enough hours in the week to do everything I want to do.

A. I get out to our barn about three or four days per week, and spend a few hours each time. Since I have three horses who are all very different, it takes me a long time to get to each one. Horses are my passion, but I do participate in some school activities, sing in the Glen Ellyn Children's Chorus, and play the piano. My parents tell me I cannot be "one dimensional," and the horses are "the icing on my cake of life."

About horses...

Q. What does "Hands high" mean?

A. "Hands high" is the unit of measure used to measure a horse. A hand is four inches (about the size of an adult's hand). A horse is measured from the ground to the highest part of its withers (the big bone connecting the neck and back of the horse).

Q. I have trouble getting my horse in from the pasture without being bothered by other horses. Can you tell me how to get him in safely?

A. The best solution would probably be to have another person watch the other horses, then close the gate for you. However, if no one else is around, you can simply outsmart the other horses (that is not that difficult to do!) by ignoring them

46

and confidently bringing your horse to the gate and getting him out. I also found that if I carry a crop in my hand, the others are less apt to "hang around."

Q. My horse is scared of some barrels that are outside our ring. Every time I go past them, he spooks. Any suggestions?

A. Sometimes horses have to be convinced that every strange object is not a "nasty old horse getter." I would suggest that you lead him up to them slowly. Then let him sniff them so he knows they won't hurt him. Next, get on him and walk him past them. If he spooks again, repeat the process until you are able to walk, trot or canter past with no problem.

People are always asking me about my horses, and I do love to talk about them…

Q. How many horses do you have? How old are they, and what are their names?

A. I know I have mentioned them in my columns, but I have three right now, and two are in foal. The mares are a seven-year-old thoroughbred named Brittany, and a three-year-old thoroughbred named Outryder. Cactus is a 14-year-old Appaloosa gelding who has a very interesting story that I am saving for a future column — so stay tuned.

Along those lines, someone else asked…

Q. I know from reading your column that you have tried almost every style of riding, but which one do you do the most?

A. I ride huntseat the most, mainly because I have discovered jumping this year. Cactus is my "main man" now because of the expected foals, but I am looking forward to working with the whole gang next summer! Incidentally, I do enjoy trail riding for fun, and then we ride Western.

Q. What breed of horse was your first horse? How old? How tall was it? What color, and what was its name? How long have you had it?

A. Actually, I have had Brittany the longest. She was five when we got her. She is a lovely bay with a black mane and tail and stands 16.2 hands high.

Q. Do any of your horses drive?

A. None of them are old enough for a license! No, none of my horses drive. But, I'd love to be able to give it a try some day, as that is one of the things I haven't been able to try yet.

And, I get questions about me and the column…

Q. Why did you start writing a horse column?

A. I subscribe to several horse magazines, and after reading them for a few months, I realized they didn't have any columns or articles that were for kids or by kids. I decided that maybe I could change that by writing one myself. Since I love both writing and riding, it was a perfect match.

12

On to the Show!

Horse show! The very words create a state of excitement and apprehension within me. The excitement part is easy to understand because, as we all know, a horse show is fun. But, have you ever had to get your horse ready for a horse show? If you have, you also know that this part can be just plain hard work. Sometimes it can be fun, too! Before I bring my horse Cactus to a show, here are a few things that I must tend to.

First, I give Cactus a good grooming. I curry all the caked mud and dirt away. Then I brush him over with hard and soft brushes, brush his mane, and pick his feet.

Then, we head over to the wash stall. The wash stall is an area with a hose and a drain designed so you can easily wash your horse. Many horses are afraid of new surroundings and Cactus is no different in this respect. But they get used to it soon enough.

Once we are there, I rinse his legs and body with lukewarm water. Then I soap him up all over very well. Did you know that there are different shampoos for different colored horses? If you like, you can even use baby shampoo. Next, I rinse him thoroughly until the soap is well washed away, then I use a sweat scraper to get the excess water off.

While Cactus is still wet, I ponytail his mane so it will lay down on the right side. Then I braid his tail in one big braid to make it curly. When I ponytail his mane, I use very small ponytails. This is a lot like taking your horse to a barber shop.

Next, I clip him with the electric clippers. First, I clip around the jaw area, getting any long hairs. Then I clip his muzzle, the hair around his eyes, his bridle path (the section between the forelock and the mane), and his ears.

After clipping, I take the ponytails out one by one and braid the mane. Then I loop them under and rubber-band them. I undo his tail and put it in a French braid. Of course, the braiding is for English, but when I show Western, I leave the ponytail in his mane and just undo and brush his tail out nicely.

Finally, for a finishing touch, I spray him with show sheen, and apply hoof-black to his hooves — horse nail polish; can you imagine that? First, I spray him all over with the sheen and rub it in with old rags. Then I do the messy part: hoof-black. I usually have black hands after this job because this stuff stains.

To keep Cactus clean during the night I put a mesh sheet on him. Then I wrap his legs. I do this to protect the bottoms of his legs from getting dirty during the night. Before I tuck him in his stall for the night, I make him promise that he will not mess up his mane and tail. Even though I bribe him with carrots, he never listens. The next day (show day) I can tell he broke his promise because of the tell-tale pieces of bedding still in his mane and tail.

Now, that doesn't sound so bad, does it? Just wait until you try it! I guarantee that it is worth all the sweat and effort when you hear your name called out for the blue ribbon!

Cactus and I win a mini event!

Cactus in Winter

13

Winter Riding

"There are some special things that you must take into consideration when the snow begins."

So far, I've written about activities you can do with your horse in good weather (summer, spring or fall), but what about horsing around in the winter? People ask me if we ride during the winter. My reply is always yes, we sure do. But there are some special things that you must take into consideration when the snow begins.

It is important that you keep your horse warm. Mother Nature takes care of most of this task for me by making my horse's (Cactus) coat grow fuzzy. This keeps his body heat in.

But sometimes it gets so cold that Mother Nature isn't enough. So I do some extra things on my own to keep Cactus warm—like keeping a blanket on him or hooding him. (When Cactus has a hood on he reminds me of Zorro.) The only problem is that there is nothing to keep his ears warm. Sometimes I wish we could put gloves on his ears and wrap a scarf around his nose!

Now that you have taken care of the "outside" of your horse, what about the inside. I spoke with our barn owner, Heidi Henry, and she told me what Aux Sable Equestrian does...and what you can do for your horse in the cold weather.

The horses get a different mix of grain during the winter. Twenty percent extra corn is mixed into the grain. Two gallons of corn oil and 100 pounds of bran is mixed into each ton of grain—WOW! Also, an average horse is expected to drink at least ten to fifteen gallons (two to three buckets) of warm water per day. The change of grain mix keeps their digestive system moving in this cold weather, and the water just keeps them warm.

Now, how do we riders survive the cold, chilly weather? First, I consider myself very lucky to be able to ride in an indoor arena when the real cold hits. This is great because it keeps the cold out and it also it keeps bad weather from disturbing your riding. During really bad weather, the only place to get a decent workout is inside.

Fortunately, most everything that you can do outdoors you can also do in an indoor arena, like jumping, which I really love! However, the indoor arena does not replace getting out and riding on the trail—I have been able to trail ride only when the ice and snow are gone from the ground. Ice and snow can be very treacherous to both you and your horse.

There are certain precautions that you should take to protect yourself as well. The first thing is that you should dress in layers instead of wearing a big heavy coat. Secondly, you can buy ear muffs that attach to your riding helmet that can make a big difference in your comfort level. Also, they now sell thermal riding gloves. These are nice because circulation to your hands is limited and they can get really cold when they are exposed for a length of time.

There are some other special things you can do for your horse when it is freezing outside. You can warm his bit by wrapping your hands tightly around it for about five minutes. Also, you can bring your horse warm apple cider and pour it into his water. You can warm his water too. Sometimes I also wish I could give them my electric blanket to use. My mom would have a fit!

Riding is a year-round activity in my house. Cactus is still there and he needs me to stick with him through thick and thin, through warm and through cold. So, stick in there with your horse all winter long. Use your head and make sure that things are as safe and comfortable as you can make them for you and your horse.

Kiki Osbourne

Baby Gene and Mom Brittany

Grown-up Gene and me

14

Breeding A Dream

Brittany was our first horse, a Thoroughbred bay mare. We thought it would be nice to breed her sometime in the future, but I never thought it would be so soon. Not knowing a thing about breeding horses, we knew we had our work cut out for us. I would like to tell you about this experience in case you ever decide to do this.

First we had to decide on a stallion. So, my mom did the logical thing — stallion interviews! I'm not sure if everyone does this, but we were very picky about our horses, so we started making phone calls and visiting farms. We felt lucky to have found Horizon Farms in Barrington, Illinois, a breeding and training facility. The staff there was very helpful and offered a lot of suggestions. It was for this reason we chose one of the stallions from that farm. It is important to be comfortable with the farm, I think, because we wanted to know <u>everything</u>!

After we moved Brittany to the farm, it took some time for her to be "in season." Then we had to see if she was "in foal." When we finally determined that by ultrasound, we found that she might have twins! Oh boy, I thought—two babies! But Sharon, the breeder, told us that twins were very dangerous for the mother and the babies may not develop properly. We had to "pinch off" one of the eggs and hope that the other one would develop. Not to worry...Brittany is a strong horse! We took her home to "wait."

Did you know that it takes about 11 months for the foal to develop? How could I stand this wait? My vet told me that I could ride her up until the last couple of months and that would keep her in shape. All I know is that she needed a girth extender after a short while!

As the foaling date grew close, we moved her back to Horizon. The "due" date came and went—still no baby! Finally, we got the call that she was going to foal soon! Of course, Brittany would do things "her" way—having the foal at suppertime and not laying down at all. They had to "catch" the foal so it didn't fall on its head!

We got to see this fine colt when he was only two hours old. He's a beautiful bay with a star and a stripe. Since his daddy was a fine racehorse, we think he might just follow in those "hoofsteps." Only time will tell. All I can say is watch your Kentucky Derby program in 1993 for "Gene's Dream." That's my dream!

This is Pony Club!

Cactus makes sure we set up the tack room
"the Pony Club way."

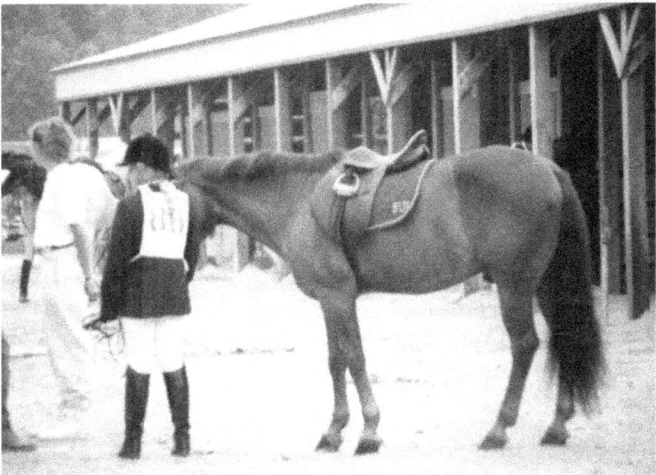

Cactus and I wait for our Formal Inspection at
Pony Club Rally

The Parade of Teams is one of my favorite parts of a Pony Club Rally

Our team worked together to win ribbons in riding and stable managemen…Alicia, Liz, Me, Martha, and Joette!

15

Pony Club Time!

One of the best-kept secrets in all of horsedom is a kids program called the PONY CLUB. Several months ago I had the good fortune of learning about the St. James Pony Club here in DuPage County, Illinois, and soon afterwards I joined.

I've enjoyed this experience so much that I figured all equikids (ages 7 to 21) should be made aware of this wonderful opportunity. I recently interviewed Mr. John Davies, manager of equestrian activities at St. James farm and the instructor of winter lessons in the Pony Club program associated with it.

I found out that the local St. James Pony Club started eight years ago when two pony clubs were going to have to disband because of lack of facilities. Mr. Davies offered to let them use St. James Farm for their meetings. At that point both clubs merged and eventually became the St. James Pony Club.

The first time I went to St. James for the lesson, I thought, "what a place!" Not only was there an excellent large indoor arena (HEATED!), but also there were top-notch instructors like Mr. and Mrs. Davies. They are both extremely knowledgeable about anything that has to do with horses. Not only that, they know how to have fun with horses, too.

During the Pony Club year, we will attend many shows and rallies. Rallies are shows where you compete as a TEAM in different events like Cross Country, Dressage and Show Jumping. Every person earns a certain number of points for each event in which he or she participates. When the dust settles, the points are added up to get a final overall score. The team with the most points naturally wins! Sounds like fun, right? I sure think so!

During the summer there is a camp especially for Pony Clubbers. At PC Camp you spend a whole week with your horse and fellow Pony Club members. I'm definitely planning to attend this year. I expect that the best part of this camp will be learning more about horsemanship from "real experts."

So how DOES one become such an expert? Judging from my conversation with Mr. Davies, it takes concentration, and a lot of plain old-fashioned work.

Mr. Davies first got into horses when he was around five. He helped a farmer deliver milk. The farmer owned a horse that he used for his deliveries. Mr. Davies groomed the horse regularly and eventually started to ride him. The farmer gave him lessons. From here on, it is history. Mr. Davies eventually taught hundreds of students per day at the London Equitation School. He also taught at the Spanish Riding School in Vienna, Austria.

Pony Club actually originated when children of fox hunters in England wanted to be able to ride in the fox hunts like their parents. The parents' response was to organize a kids' club that eventually became the Pony Club of today.

The truly unique thing is that Pony Club is the only INTERNATIONAL riding association that exists strictly for children. What an opportunity to have the chance to meet kids from all over the world who share one common bond — LOVE OF HORSES!

Pony Club is a very exciting experience for me. It's a chance to increase my knowledge of horses and riding. I discovered that one of the main objectives of Pony Club is to develop good SAFETY habits around our four legged friends. I would sure like to see a lot of other kids get involved with this fun and educational activity.

Pony Clubs around the country are always looking for new members. I personally guarantee you an equispecial good time!

Did you know that there are over 600 Pony Clubs nationwide (including Alaska and Hawaii), more than 13,000 members, and thousands of volunteers! Members range in age from as young as 4, up to 21. And, don't let the name fool you...members don't just ride ponies, although many of the younger members do. Older members ride horses, too!

To find out more about the United States Pony Clubs, and how you can get in on the fun, contact them at 4041 Iron Works Parkway, Lexington, KY, 40511-8483. Phone: 859-254-7669. Or, visit their website at www.ponyclub.org.

Kiki Osbourne

At the Schooling Show...Torey, me and Shannon

16

Planning An Equispecial Schooling Show

I know that many of you have attended and participated in horse shows, but how many have had the opportunity to plan and organize one? Recently I had the opportunity — lucky me — and I would like to tell you all about it. When the idea first came up, I thought that organizing a horse show would be easy. All I had to do was make a show bill and ride my horse — right? But organizing a show was a lot more work than I expected.

For example, my mom said that it wouldn't do much good to have a show if we didn't tell anyone about it. So, we decided to organize a publicity campaign. We made lots of signs that gave the date, place and time, etc. We hung them on bulletin boards with all the rest of the notices.

I made a lot of colorful signs and banners on my home computer (but kept forgetting to bring them to the barn to hang them up). We talked about doing a mailing, but we didn't have enough money. We also talked about calling everyone on the phone, but we didn't have enough time. But, finally we thought that the signs would suffice, and we let it go at that.

Another thing that we had to plan were the awards. All horse shows have awards of some kind, so we decided that we had to have some, too. We called a bunch of ribbon dealers and got their catalogs. For a while we were set on getting 12 sets of stock ribbons which were very nice and cheap— inexpensive, I mean.

Then our plans changed, because even these ribbons were going to cost more money than we could afford. So we managed to scrounge up some old ribbons that were left over from last season and used them for our show. I ordered champion and reserve champion ribbons, because we were planning to recognize hi-point and reserve hi-point winners. I also ordered 25 certificates with horses on them for first and second place. For third through sixth place I made certificates on my computer.

As you can tell by now, we were trying to manage this event on a shoestring. For judging, we knew Barb Richardson, an amateur equine judge in the area. She said that she would work our event just to gain the experience. She was very nice to us, and she did a wonderful job of judging our contestants.

I was also responsible for creating our show bill. After we decided the logical order of the classes, I put this information up on my computer (it turned out great), and had my mom make a bunch of copies at her office.

The publicity, the awards, the judging, and the show bills were all planned in advance. But, interestingly enough, there were also a few things that we didn't plan for. And this is where the whole thing got a little tricky.

The day of the show, we found that we didn't have any numbers for the contestants. So, I dug up some construction paper, cut them into rectangles, and put the numbers on with black Magic Marker (improvise, improvise).

Then we discovered that we had neglected to recruit an announcer. Much to her dismay, we roped my mom into being our announcer. She told me afterwards that this was the first time she was ever able to ask me to do something once—and have me comply. I think that she was exaggerating—but, maybe not.

The moral of this story is, if you ever decide to organize a horse show, be prepared to put in a lot of work. Organization is the key word. Make a list: publicity, show bills, awards, refreshments, logistics, numbers, judges, announcers, cashiers, ribbon giver-outers, etc. Then, be prepared to be surprised a few times, too. But, if you can pull it off, planning and organizing a horse show can be an equispecial experience.

Brittany

17

Equispecial Brittany

For seven long months I've been waiting for Brittany, my first horse, to come "home" from Horizon Thoroughbred Farm. She had a foal in April and stayed with him until he was weaned. Almost every day I dreamed up new goals and ideas for this reunited team—Brittany and me. I circled items in catalogs and ordered things from tack shops I thought she had to have. Let's face it. I missed her and talked about her constantly to anyone who would listen. I built up her reputation until people were wondering if they *really* wanted to meet this infamous animal. You see, she has always been a wonderful horse under saddle, but her ground manners left a lot to be desired.

Finally, on a Thursday night, around two weeks ago, a van full of our friends (it was kind of like a welcome wagon) drove to Horizon to pick up Brittany. All the way there I was wondering if motherhood had changed her at all. I had been visiting her from time to time, but I had not been "close" to her in a long time. I thought about some of the problems we might have: loading, clipping, and saddling. These were things I had come to take for granted with my other horse, Cactus.

After a long struggle of trying to get her into the trailer, she finally went in. (There was my answer to the first question about loading!) We were on our way home! YES!

The next day I wanted to ride her and had to face the other problem of saddling. She really surprised me and didn't rear up as usual. I was even able to mount without her dancing around too much. She was a little skittish at first, but after a while she calmed down. One problem was that she put her nose in the air all the time. I decided to take care of that with some draw reins. She is quick to learn, and she tucked her head and collected up, just like the "old days."

One last problem we had with her was cross-tying and tying her up. She has managed to break halters and cross-ties in the past by rearing. This was a fact I neglected to tell our farrier when he came out that first week. Much to our surprise (and lucky for him), he tied her, and she was very good. I have also begun to treat her like any other horse, and tie her.

I found that, in our case, motherhood was good for our horse. She sure seemed to be much calmer and accepting of things. However, I must say that she probably doesn't know that I have changed as well. I am no longer the young, inexperienced rider she first knew. I spent the last year with Pony Club working on my horsemanship and horse handling with my good ol' buddy, Cactus. It looks like we're off to a good, new start. Welcome home, Brittany, my friend!

Kiki Osbourne

Magnetic and me

18

Magnetic's Attraction

One of the things I'd like to do when I get out of school is to ride horses professionally. Did you know that people actually hire riders to show a horse in horse shows? I had my first opportunity to get an idea of what this would be like when my friend Marcy asked me if I wanted to work with her and show her horse, Magnetic, in some shows this summer.

I started my career with Magnetic back in October. When I first found out about it I was very excited. First of all, he's a gray, my favorite color. Second, he's calm and steady. It was exciting to ride such a fine horse, and a bit scary at the same time, since Marcy has been virtually the only one to ride him for the past eight years. I knew it would be a challenge just to get to know Magnetic, and for us to learn to trust each other.

So, from then on, every week I went out to ride Magnetic. I was surprised to find out how smooth he was. I hardly bounced in the saddle. I thought he was sure a lot different from my horse Cactus, who has a short and choppy stride. Magnetic is very light on his feet, while Cactus plods along, seeming to dread every step of the way.

I was surprised that I got to take him over a jump the first day. Magnetic galloped towards the jump, and I about fell off, totally not expecting him to fly as he did. Marcy told me he cleared the low jump with about two feet to spare, something I was definitely not used to, as Cactus seems to always take the most efficient jump possible, laying low and close to the jump. My Mom said that "Maggie" looks like he has radar in his ears, and zeroes in on every jump he sees.

I found myself looking forward to those weekly sessions with Magnetic, and as time went on, we became friends. I think he knows me now, although I know Marcy is his "first love." We figured he would get used to me fairly easily because both Marcy and I have blonde hair!

Soon we felt I was ready to "do a course" with Maggie. Now this was a new ball game for me. In doing a course we had to concentrate on not only getting over the jumps, but having the correct leads, and MOST IMPORTANTLY, *REMEMBERING* the course! After a while, I found that if I let Magnetic "do his thing," I only needed to guide him correctly — sure removes some pressure. (Thank you, Magnetic.)

Right now we are looking over the summer show offerings, and trying to pick some shows for us to attend. We already participated in one a few weeks ago — I call that our "warm-up." Maggie and I placed in every class, although the team of Marcy/Magnetic cleaned up with a Championship in their division.

"Oh well," I thought, "I guess I need a few more years of experience."

For now, I am happy to be working with Magnetic. Someday, I hope to be able to ride many more like him. For the moment, I am enjoying the magic of Magnetic, spreading his wings, and flying over the jumps.

Cactus and I demonstrate jumping

19

Danada Open House

Several years ago, before I ever started riding horses, I went on a Girl Scout field trip to a new DuPage County Forest Preserve called Danada Equestrian Center. I still remember the fun we had touring the farm, going on a hay ride, and best of all, seeing the horse demonstrations. After that, I was "hooked" on horses, and shortly thereafter, I started riding.

For those of you who don't know about Danada, and for those of you who know of it, but have not had a chance to see it, I would like to tell you about its recent "open house," hoping you will get to know Danada for yourself someday.

Danada is an equestrian facility that is on the West side of DuPage County, south of Butterfield Road on Naperville Road. Danada was once the home of Dan and Ada Rice (thus the name Danada) who were breeders and racers of thoroughbred horses.

The Rices owned the 1965 Kentucky Derby winner, Lucky Debonaire, and Willie Shoemaker was the jockey! Then the Rices passed away, the DuPage County Forest preserve bought their estate and turned it into a horse rehabilitation and equestrian center.

At the annual open house, Danada displays various breeds of horses, types of riding and horse care techniques. Being a member of St. James Pony Club, I was invited to participate in a show jumping demonstration this year, an opportunity I only dreamed about a few years earlier.

So, early Saturday morning, I went to my barn to get my horse Cactus ready for the big day. Since my barn is only about a half a mile from Danada, I rode over. As soon as I arrived, a hostess greeted me and gave me a few guest passes and a schedule. She seemed genuinely happy to see me and made me feel welcome and part of the Danada family for the day.

I was directed to a stall in the "big barn," and before I could even begin to get Cactus situated, I was flooded with questions from an entire Girl Scout troop and their leaders. "What's his name? What breed of horse is he? Do you ride him English or Western?" I enjoyed answering all the questions, and smiled to myself, remembering that only a few short years ago it was *me*, asking those same questions!

After a while two other people came up to me and asked, "Is this Cactus?" I wondered how they knew my horse? Then they introduced themselves as Cactus'ss former owners, the Lawlers. They told me some things about Cactus that I didn't know before, like his birth date! After this informative chat, I walked Cactus to his "stall for a day." He was in heaven because he could stick his head out of the stall and get petted.

Then I went out to watch some of the wonderful demonstrations. I saw musical longeing (when a handler works a horse on a line, in a circle, for training or exercise) and I saw a quadrille team do a routine. There were also driving demonstrations with the horses all decked out in bows. All of them were so well planned and so well executed that it made them great fun to watch.

While I tacked up, several kids came up to me asking about Cactus'ss saddle, bridle and splint boots. I answered all of their questions as well as I could. A number of kids asked if my saddle was Western or English. I explained that a Western saddle was big, and it had a horn, while an English saddle was smaller and had no horn. So, mine was an English saddle.

It was finally my turn to demonstrate show jumping. I warmed up Cactus, and we started over some low X's and worked our way up to a 2'6" jump. As we rode over the fences, the announcer explained the two-point jumping position, the approach, the take-off, suspension, the landing and the get away of show jumping. I was thinking to myself all the while, "keep your eyes up, heels down, and keep Cactus going smoothly over the fences."

We went through the course about five times and had lots of fun. As we walked back to the big barn, I got lots of compliments from all the kids in the audience. I sure hope that I get to demonstrate at Danada again next year.

If Dan and Ada Rice were here today, they would be happy to know that Danada was being used for such a wonderful purpose. If you haven't been to Danada yourself, take the time...it's well worth the effort!

20

An Equispecial Summer Camp

While other kids were spending a week or so at summer camps in canoes or doing arts and crafts projects, I was at a very "horsey" camp. This unique camp was the St. James Pony Club Camp. I would like to tell you about my experiences, and maybe next summer you might consider a "horse" type camp.

Instead of packing my sleeping bag and pillow, I was packing hay and oats for my horse Cactus. But, I didn't care—I was very excited about this equine camp. After all, Cactus and I were going to spend every day for a week at St. James farm!

Although the camp officially started on Monday, we were to arrive Sunday night to drop off our horses and get them settled in to what was to be their home for the next week. (Lucky Ducks...I mean, HORSES!!) As is the case with most camps (as all of you experienced campers know), we were assigned teams. I was happy to be on the "Lipizzan" team. We had to work together to get the hay and tack room ready. That accomplished, I fed Cactus, put him to bed, and went home to get everything else ready for the next day.

I think the hardest part about camp was getting up so early to go to St. James and get Cactus fed early enough so he would have time to digest his food before we started the daily activities. On the first day we were given the daily schedules, which remained the same for the entire week.

Study groups were the first on our group's agenda. In Pony Club, KNOWLEDGE and SAFETY are at the top of the list, with riding, of course, being a part of the activities. We learned about the horse's legs and the bones in them. Other topics covered were the dressage arena, loading, and longeing. Did you know that you should always put a bridle on a horse when you longe them? I never knew that before Pony Club Camp.

After study groups we saddled up and rode, most often in the dressage arena. We worked on some drill team stunts that taught us coordination and communication between horse and rider. Then we were ready for work on our dressage test. I believe I learned a lot in this class, because I never really had done a dressage test before.

Of course, we did take time out to eat a quick lunch, then it was back to work. Actually, it really didn't seem like work at all. After all, how many times does one have the opportunity to spend so much time with friends who all have HORSES in common?!?

We had a second session of study groups in the afternoon, then more riding. We concentrated on different things each time, so we were never bored. My favorite was the "nursery," which is a fenced-in, Cross Country course for schooling young horses and riders before they actually go out on a real Cross Country course. There were a variety of jumps such a log piles, verticals, coops, and small drops. I even learned how not to lean too far back or forward over and down a drop.

After the final ride of the day, we had informal learning groups that helped us perfect such skills as braiding and wrapping. The final chore was feeding and cleaning stalls before we were allowed to go home for the day. Even that was fun, because the entire "lipizzan" team pitched in.

I would say that when you're making summer camp plans next year, consider taking your horse to camp. I know I will!

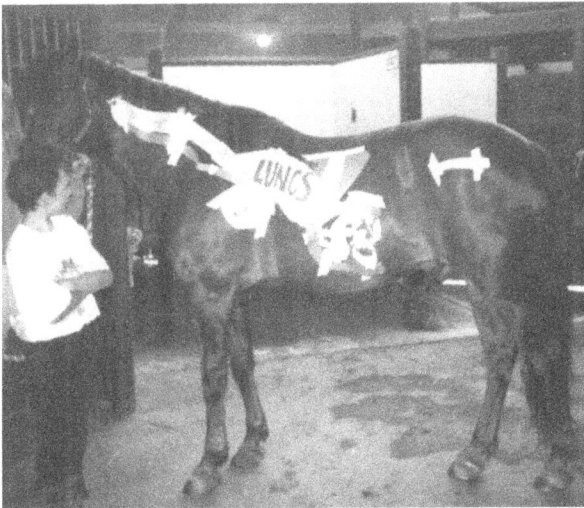

Cactus, helping at Pony Club Camp

"All I want for Christmas…"

21

Equispecial Christmas Gift Ideas

'Tis the season to be jolly...even in horse country. Over the past year, I have written about everything from different styles of riding to 4-H meetings and "getting ready for the show." But, when the Christmas season rolls around, I get sentimental, and I find myself wanting to talk about the true meaning of Christmas-PRESENTS!

Actually, this article is about giving, rather than receiving. That is, I would like to give you some hints (equine) for your Christmas shopping this year.

If you are shopping for friends at your barn, there is a wide variety of gifts to choose from. One of the newest equine gifts on the market is "horse cards." Horse cards are a new kind of trading card (like baseball cards) for the young horse lover. You might also consider horse posters, or model horses (like my Breyer horses) for your friend. I know that would be something I'd like for Christmas (hint, hint). For a friend who likes to read, you could give him a subscription to his favorite horse magazine.

Next, your stable owner is someone else you would probably love to cheer up, since he tends to your horse with tender, loving care on a daily basis. New tools would be a nice idea. I'm sure he/she could always use something to help him/her clean the stable. The best present for your stable owner, though, would probably be a new boarder or two. So, if you have any ideas along this line. I'm sure that you could brighten his holiday.

Now, for your four-legged friends (with hoofs): The best present you could give them, that is, the gift they would enjoy most, would be carrots, apples or sugar. A very nice present that wouldn't cost you very much is a special grooming. Your friend would probably enjoy that. You could even hang stockings on your horse's stall (with carrots) in hopes that Santa Horse will soon be there.

For those of you who don't yet have a real horse of your own, you might want to buy a gift or two for your Breyer horses. I have been checking out the Christmas gift market for these guys, too. A few of the things that I have run across include saddles that would fit many of the Breyers. There are bridles of all sorts with bits that range from snaffles to kimberwicks. I also found blankets in all colors and sizes, and even splint and skid boots that fit perfectly on a Breyer's tiny leg.

Finally, for a horse-crazy person such as me, I really enjoy getting new tack for my horses. I would like a new show saddle, since I have three horses and only one saddle. I would also enjoy a few more Breyer model horses to add to my already overpopulated model collection. Another nice gift that I would like is a lucky horseshoe to take to horse shows. I can always use more luck, you know. The thing that I always want most is another horse of my own, even though I know I won't get one this year.

As you and your family (including your horses) get caught up in the spirit of Christmas, don't forget the clicking of little hoofs and your horse's joyful whinny. Yes Virginia, even the horse world looks forward to Christmas. Until next year, then, I would like to wish everyone out there in horse land an *Equispecial Christmas and an Equispecial New Year* as well!

Kiki Osbourne

My perfect stick horse!

The Third Year

Kiki Osbourne

"Racehorse in Progress"

22

Buying an Equispecial Race Horse

How many of you have ever bought a racehorse? Not too many, right? I have a friend named Jim who owns racehorses, and he took me with him on a buying trip several weeks ago. I had so much fun that I decided to tell you all about it.

Jim had an early morning appointment, so we all got up at 7:00 a.m. (during vacation, even!) and arrived at the track by 8:00 a.m. Jim shook hands with the trainer and asked him to show us a horse named Zip Plus Four.

Before we even saw Zip, we looked at a couple of other horses this trainer had in training. The barns at the track have surprisingly a lot more room than one might think. The aisles are wide enough to walk and even ride horses through! As we walked through the maze of stalls, there were tons of horses getting cooled down and hand-walked through the barns. All the while we were there, we saw them go around and around and around and around and...Anyway, we finally got to see "THE HORSE."

Before our very eyes stood a big red chestnut colt. His big, dark eyes stared at us in curiosity. After we patted him a while, he decided we weren't going to hurt him. (Darn, I had forgotten my carrots!) Soon he was nipping at us and being his playful self. Joel, one of Jim's friends who knew a lot about racehorses, checked his legs for any problems. He said that nothing seemed to be wrong. Jim fell in love with him and HAD to buy him. A vet came out and checked him and said he was sound. In the meantime, Zip ran in a race and was watched closely to see how he did. Even though he didn't finish "in the money," Jim and his friend still thought he might be a good addition to their stable.

A few days later, Jim went back to the track and bought him. Since all the horses had to leave Hawthorne Race Track for the end of the season, Jim arranged to have him shipped to Horizon farms, the breeding and training facility where we had our mares. Everybody at Horizon seemed to like him.

Just yesterday, we took a trip to Horizon to take "family" pictures of Zip. Since I am the official photographer in our family, I was elected to do the honors. We started by opening the top of his stall door and had him peek out at us for a few photos. Then it was time to take him out. We were sure glad to have Dave from Horizon around to handle this fellow, as he was very "hot" when we took him out. He reared and bucked for about 10 minutes. Finally he calmed down enough for us to take pictures. We were careful not to get too close, as he was striking out at close bodies. After all he was in a strange place, with strange people, and he really didn't know us yet.

After the photo session, we headed back to the office at Horizon to warm up and have some birthday cake. Did you know that all thoroughbreds have their official birthday on January 1? We brought out a celebration cake that said "Happy Birthday to All the Horses at Horizon Farms." Of course, we humans got to enjoy it, but we did wish the horses Happy Birthday. Maybe next time we'll bring extra carrots for them!

Now, I can't wait until the next racing season. I can just hear it now: "And to the wire in first place, Zip Plus Four." I can say, "I know that horse." I always thought the racing world was boring. After all, how much fun can it be to only WATCH horses being ridden? I want to be riding! But NOW it will be exciting with Zip-A-Dee-Do-Dah Stable's new addition. Welcome, Zip!

Copper

23

Equispecial Mailbag II

During 1990, I collected several questions asked of me from people who have read my column in Bit & Bridle, and I would like to share some of these with you this month.

Q. *Why do horses crib? Windsuck?*

A. Horses crib, (a vice where a horse bites and holds on to wood, buckets, whatever it can get its teeth on) or windsuck, (A vice where a horse sucks in air while biting wood) mostly because of boredom. My horse, Outryder, cribs and windsucks. We have tried everything to stop her. But she finds a way to crib anyway. I am hoping that she returns home to our barn soon so I can keep her VERY BUSY working! Then maybe she won't have any "spare" time on her hands.

Q. *Why do horses refuse jumps?*

A. Horses refuse jumps for a few reasons. One is lack of training. A horse may not understand that you want him to JUMP that hay bale in front of him, rather than eat it. One of the first times I tried to jump my horse, Cactus, he stopped dead and proceeded to EAT the jump! Another reason could be lameness. Always check out your horse VERY carefully before jumping. Your horse knows that it would be in pain if it had to jump with a sore leg.

Q. How often do a horse's feet need to be trimmed?

A. A horse's feet should be trimmed at least every six weeks. Their feet could overgrow the shoe they have on and it could be very painful. It also depends upon the work your horse is doing. Sometimes the shoes will wear out faster, or he may throw a shoe, or his hoof may grow at a different rate of speed.

Q. Why does your horse need regular vet check-ups?

A. Regular vet check-ups are necessary because your horse could have injured something and you may not detect it. Also, your horse needs to get his immunizations every few months to protect him from disease, worms, etc.

Q. How should a good saddle fit your horse?

A. You should be able to see down the middle of the saddle, lengthwise, on your horse's back. Also, you should be able to fit about a hand around the wither bone.

The Kiki Chronicles:
An Equispecial Journey

Q. How often do you ride in the winter?

A. I ride every other day and sometimes more, if I can convince my mom to take me out to the barn! I work my horses in the arena during the week, and on the weekends I head out on the trails, if there is no ice on the trail. So, they get about five days of work a week.

Q. Why do you need warm-ups?

A. Warm-ups are necessary because when you take a horse right from his stall its muscles are not stretched out or loosened up. So, you gradually increase the pace of your horse from a walk to a trot to a canter. Around 10-15 minutes of warm-up (and even more sometimes) is sufficient. You should check with your trainer for the schedule that is best for your horse.

Q. What is the maximum height of a Western or English pony?

A. A Western and English pony should be 14.2 hands and under.

Q. How tall is the tallest horse?

A. You got me on that one! Do any of you readers know how tall is the tallest horse, and WHO it is? I would like to know, and I'm sure others would as well. I will do some research and let you know what I find out!

Q. What color are your two foals?

A. Gene's Big Dream is a bay colt with a star and a stripe. Magic Ryder is a chestnut filly with a star. Please look for them in the 1993 Kentucky Derby Program!

This has been fun "chatting" with you all. If anyone has more questions, please let me know, and I will try to answer them either by mail or in my column again in the future.

24

Walking on A Winter Wonder Trail

Even though it's very cold outside, trail rides through the woods are still A LOT of fun. Last week it snowed a lot. Tons of trees were covered in snow. My friend Torey and I saddled up my faithful friend, Cactus, for a snowy ride.

As we walked up the hill, we saw only a huge blanket world of snow. Everything glistened like fairy dust. It looked like snow sculptors were turned loose to build snow trees in the woods, for all the trees were white. Each tree had its own different shape and had been finished up to the last end of the littlest branch. The trails were clearly marked by a smooth line of snow only to be disturbed by the hoofs of many fleet deer and a lone, tired horse.

My friend and I were riding Cactus double and every time we'd turn our heads we'd start oohing and aahing. It was as if every living thing was somehow magically turned into a master work of art. Finally we had reached the river. What a sight! White willow trees hung over the murky dark river. Snow caves lay around it, and made it look like it flowed on for miles under the snow. The river, so black, looked like a bottomless pit of darkness. The trees reflected off the slow-flowing river. A lonely ice chunk floated by, assuring us we were still standing, looking at the river.

As we retreated home following the deer trails, marked by their tracks, darkness fell, but magically, nothing seemed to get dark. Cactus's chestnut coat against the snow made him only a mere shadow that accented this lovely picture. Total silence. No birds chirped. No wind blew. The only sound was the pleasant sound of Cactus's hooves crunching over the snow.

Torey and I decided we should break this silence and hum a well-known Christmas carol. Singing in harmony, we completed the picture. A snow world, a horse, two riders, singing a carol. That's just how I always pictured horseback riding to be. Everything always in the right spot at the right time. Unfortunately this can't always be true. But it's great while it lasts!

25

Yee Hah!!!

For the past five years or so, I've been riding English for the most part. I've ridden saddle seat, huntseat, dressage and have been jumping, both stadium and Cross Country. Once in a while I haul out the old Western saddle that came along with my horse, Cactus, and ride a few Western classes in a show, or just hit the trails for a leisurely ride. One might say that I have had a chance to sample a large part of the equestrian scene.

Recently, I took a trip to see my best friend, Torey, who recently moved to Missouri, where Western is "the only way to ride." I thought I'd hate it there, but actually it was quite fun to be in a "Western World." Torey keeps her English Thoroughbred at an all Western Quarter horse barn. The man who owns it, Mr. McMillan, herds cattle with his Quarter horses. He was a few "heads" short the week-end I happened to be there, so he invited Torey and me to come and move the cattle with him. (Gee, just like in the movies!)

My first reaction was, "I'll be on a strange horse, riding a different style than I'm used to, and doing something I've never tried." Of course I said YES!! I couldn't stand looking at all those horses and not being able to ride them. We explained to Mr. McMillan that I rode A LOT, so he told me I could ride their Quarter horse stud, Flit-N-Freckles. I was told that Flit was a great "cuttin'" horse and was very much at home around the cows. That scared me—the HORSE knew more than I did about this job!

The next morning we saddled up the trusty steeds and got prepared to "cut the cattle." Flit looked like a very good and gentle horse that would take care of me, and it turned out that he was all that and more. I wasn't quite sure what to expect, because most of the stallions I have been around have either been a handful or under control in the dressage arena! We all mounted our horses and were off. It felt really weird to be sitting in that Western saddle with the big horn, as opposed to a flat English saddle. Flit and I seemed to get along fine.

When we arrived at the cow pasture, all sixty-six pairs of eyes stared at us. Mr. McMillan explained that if we blocked the vision of a roaming cow, they would follow the rest of the herd. The gate to the pasture was opened, and we were off to work. Using the techniques Mr. McMillan explained to us, we got the cows quickly to the next pasture. A few cows decided to climb through barbed wire fences to get away. I was amazed that it didn't seem to bother them to get stuck in the wire. While Mr. McMillan chased those cows, he left Torey and me "in charge."

Luckily no cows decided to escape from us, because we didn't know what we were doing, and they never suspected a thing!

We also sorted bulls, which a little more challenging because they didn't cooperate at all. Lesson number 2! However, Flit knew what he was doing, so I let him do his stuff while I hung on for the ride.

Finally, our work around the farm was finished. We unsaddled after a GREAT day. I found that Western riding can have as much variety as English, and that it is really fun, exciting and challenging.

I never thought that my equestrian experience would lead me to a "roundup." When I got home, I was inspired to ride my horse, Cactus, Western for a while. I even found myself checking around for stray cattle—but none wander our forest preserves these days! I guess I've done it all now—from Saddleseat to "cuttin'." Then, again, who knows where my next vacation will take me...

Trying to stay in line…Martha, me and Lynn

26

An Equispecial Drill Team

Eyes up! Keep even with your partner! Close up! Those were repetitive commands given by Mr. John Davies, who coordinated the St. James Pony Club Drill Team at our summer riding camp. Everyone was told that we would have a great time doing this activity, but what we were doing wasn't what WE had in mind for a camp activity!

Nevertheless, every day after lunch, 24 riders tacked up their trusty steeds to have a special drill team lesson. We learned a total of six basic moves. They all seemed fairly simple to learn if you concentrated. I have to admit, I messed up quite a lot because I was concentrating on other things.

One of the first things we did was to move at a walk down the middle of the arena in pairs and at the end we divided off left and right, forming two different lines directly across from each other. The next move, which I liked the best, was the twenty meter circle with two lines going different directions and passing right shoulder to right shoulder. In my opinion, this move was the best because it looked like a big wheel.

Then, keeping our horses in the same two lines, we moved diagonally across the field, passing through every other horse in the middle. Confusing, huh? After those moves were mastered at the walk, we put it all together at the sitting trot. It was hard because you really had to be aware of everyone (people AND horses!) around you to know exactly where you were supposed to be.

Then we rode down the center in "fours" and "eights." (That is, four or eight horses moving abreast) With all of these moves complete, we thought we were doing pretty good. THEN...we found we had to do all of this at the trot, and the SITTING TROT at that! This was a lot more difficult now, because all of the horses moved at different speeds and now we had to concentrate on keeping up with our partner, along with three to seven more animals too!

After three days of practice it was time to perform for our parents. We put a routine together using many of our newly acquired moves, arranging the horses according to color and size, and all this had to be done...to music!

Classical music was played over the loudspeaker as 24 riders and horses marched into the arena at a sitting trot. Amazingly, we performed all our moves well. Maybe it was the music — the horses acted as if they were dancing to the music. They actually seemed to step in time to the beat. What a picture! They loved it...we loved it...parents loved it too! What more could you ask of life?

Learning About Eventing!
(Cactus and me)

Dressage

Cross Country

Stadium

Cactus, Sundance, Mary Ruth and I are thrilled after completing our first Mini event!

27

Olympic Dreamin' at My First Mini Event

My horse-crazy friends and I have naturally dreamed of making the Olympic Equestrian team someday. You've seen it—dressage (prim, proper, precise), Cross Country (racing through the woods at break-neck speeds, jumping large logs, ponds, up and down high banks), and stadium jumping (jumping unbelievable heights with precision timing).

I began my quest for the dream by recently participating in a mini-event at TLC (Team Laura Clarkson.) Different from a horse show where one might enter eight or ten classes, the mini-event allows the participant to have three rides: Dressage, Cross Country, and Stadium Jumping. Also different is the fact that you do not have to wait around all day wondering when your class will go in the arena. You are assigned "ride times," and I found out that you'd better be there when assigned, or you lose your chance to ride!

All last year my friends from St. James Pony Club were telling me how much fun mini-events were, but I just could not fit any into my summer schedule. So, at the beginning of this show season, I told myself I had to attend a mini-event this year. So two weeks ago, we finally headed to TLC in Elgin.

As with any other horse show, the day started out at 6:00 a.m. at the barn where my friend Mary and I braided our horses. Cactus was being very uncooperative, and it took quite a while to braid him. That gave us time to talk about what was ahead of us for the day. Mary was nervous because this was the first real event she'd ever attended. I told her there was nothing to worry about, because we were just doing it for fun.

We *finally* loaded the horses and arrived at TLC only about fifteen minutes before Mary's dressage test began and twenty minutes before mine. Our parents helped by tacking up the horses while we got ourselves ready. Within ten minutes we were on the horses and riding up to the dressage arena, wondering if we could squeeze in a *quick* warm-up somewhere.

The beginning of the dressage phase was different from a normal dressage test. Instead of going around the outside of the ring for 90 seconds, we rode directly into the arena because the dressage arena was indoors. We found that to be different, but helpful, too, because it gave the horses a chance to see inside the arena. My dressage went very nicely. As a matter of fact, I was holding tight to second place after this event. Mary wound up in third place and was very happy with her performance as well. One down.

We knew then that we would at least get a ribbon for our dressage. Generally at an event, ribbons are awarded on *total* performance and, if a participant has a lot of faults or is eliminated in any of the three phases, he would be "out of the ribbons." However, at this mini-event, ribbons are awarded for dressage, *and* overall points.

According to our ride time assignment, we had about two hours until Cross Country started. That gave us just enough time to relax and to walk the course and plan our strategy for each obstacle. The course was short—only eleven jumps. None of them were over 2'6", and none were very difficult. There were two small banks that I liked best. When we came back from walking the course, we tacked up and put splint boots and bell boots on our horses. We also had to get ourselves ready. I had to put on my jumping vest—for safety's sake, not to mention that my mom insisted on it!

We were schooling our horses for about fifteen minutes, when we looked around and saw that everyone had removed the braids from their horses' manes. Mmmmm. This was telling us something...remove those braids quickly...we need some mane to hang onto as we fly over all those jumps! So, Mary and I very quickly removed braids, without ever getting off the horses' backs! Very soon after, our numbers were called. I saw Mary start out of the starting gate trotting her horse most of the way because she (Mary) had never experienced a Cross Country course before. In the end she finished up with only one refusal. Pretty good for the first time!

When it was our turn, Cactus got all excited about running Cross Country. When the timer said, "go" we cantered out of the starting area and flew over the first jump. He cantered the remainder of the course and jumped everything cleanly. So, after Cross Country we were still in second place. I was very pleased with Cactus's performance. Two down.

Now the last big challenge was the stadium phase. At my last event I was eliminated in stadium (three refusals), and I wanted to be sure to avoid an instant replay of that experience. We all saddled up for stadium and schooled while we watched the other riders perform their feats. The champion horse in the first division was awarded a blue ribbon which was placed around his neck. His rider also won a big first place ribbon and looked very proud.

By this time I knew that if Cactus went clean, and the first place horse at this point didn't, *we* would win first place. I could just picture Cactus with that ribbon around his neck. But, enough dreaming...back to the task at hand.

Luckily, our trainer, Kathy Kelly, happened to be there competing as well, and she gave Mary and me several last-minute tips. Suddenly, it was Mary's turn. She and Mr. Tuck had a super round, with no faults. All too soon it was my turn. Cactus flew over all the jumps, and we finished clean, too. I could only hug him and tell him how great he was. Three down! Done!

Now all I had to do was wait and see how the first place horse did. Off she went, and at the first jump the horse refused. Then, at the second jump, the horse refused again. They finished clean the rest of the way, but by that time I could predict the final positions.

Finally, the winners were ready to be announced. "In first place overall and second after dressage…Kendra Osbourne on "Lost my Spots" (that's Cactus'ss show name), the announcer proclaimed. "And, in third place and third after Dressage…Mary Ruth Joy on Mr. Tuck," he added. What a day! We were both ecstatic!

At an event, the winners take a victory gallop around the course, and I got to lead the gallop. It was really exciting to be leading a group of competitors like this around the arena. Best of all, I had fun the whole day. I've already planned to take another horse to a mini-event in September. It will be good practice for both of us. Today TLC, tomorrow the Olympics…You never know.

Kiki Osbourne

"Western and English"

28

An Equispecial Team Tournament

A few weeks ago, I participated in a unique 4-H horse show called Team Tournament. Different from a regular open show where we compete AGAINST each other, here we compete WITH each other as a 4-H club team.

Five of us planned to compete, not knowing what a team tournament actually was. But, it was an opportunity to show our horses and learn something new. Our team (Mary Ruth Joy, John Joy, Amy Leach, Liz Nelson, and myself) expected team tournament to be a rather small show, but we were wrong. Tons of clubs showed up, from several counties. When we pulled in, the whole area for trailer parking was almost full. We knew then that our competition would be tough. It was also supposed to be really hot, so everyone took it easy, and decided that we would just enjoy the day.

Here is how the tournament worked. We would compete as a team, earning team points by our placement in each class. We would receive no ribbons for these placements, and the points would be cumulative. The team with the highest points at the end of the show wins. The contestants would be divided into two age groups, 13 and under, and 14 thru 18. What we didn't know was that there were two divisions: large and small clubs.

The day started off like the usual horse show with only two halter classes, unlike the normal average of ten. I took Cactus in the very crowded showmanship class. Cactus and I didn't place, but Liz and her horse, Contessa, placed fourth. We were happy with that because it meant points for our team. The next classes were bareback classes. In the younger division, Amy and Mary Ruth placed second and sixth, while I placed sixth in the older division. Aha…more points.

Only three of us were planning to compete in the English classes. The good thing about this team tournament is that everyone has a chance to contribute to the team no matter what their riding specialty is. In English Equitation, Cactus did everything very well as usual and I guess I looked pretty good because I came out with second place. I was very pleased. Amy got a third in equitation and Mary got a fifth. We were all very excited. In my pleasure class, I got a fifth. Cactus thought he should have done better, but, oh well! Amy and Mary also placed in pleasure.

Finally we got to do jumping—the best part of the day, in my opinion. Mary did her round first on her pony Sundance. She finished with a fifth, and I finished with a second in my division. At the end of the English class we felt our team was doing very well.

After lunch they had the Western classes. Four of us competed in this phase. I started with the trail class and Cactus surprised me and did everything he was supposed to. Because of that, we came out with a surprising fourth. We all rode in the pleasure classes, but no one placed and earned any points in that division.

The most exciting part of the day was next—gaming (barrels, poles and flags). Four of us planned to compete, but we all knew this wasn't our specialty. We just knew it was fun to do. First we did flags. For those of you who don't know what this is: You grab a flag from one barrel on one side of the arena and race to the other side and put it in a bucket of sand which is sitting on top of another barrel. The winner, of course, is the person who can do that feat the fastest. That's my favorite game because it's the only one that has no tight turns and I can gain speed. However, only Mary earned points for our team on that one!

Following the flag race were barrels. Mary did very well, but went too close and knocked over a barrel. Darn! Cactus wouldn't cut close enough, so our time was not very good, but we managed to squeeze out a sixth place. Speedy John and his horse Justice, ended up with a fourth, once again earning points for the team. Everyone enjoyed watching the barrel racing because some of the kids specialized in barrels and had tremendous speed. People were fascinated at how fast a horse could go around something.

The last race we did was poles. We had to run down to one end of the arena, weave through a line of poles twice and run back. Cactus normally does these very well, but unfortunately, on our initial run, his curb bit flipped in his mouth and I couldn't turn him to his first pole, so I was eliminated, much to my disappointment. Oh well, we ended up with only Mary placing in the games.

With that complete, we headed back to the stabling area to get untacked. As we were cooling off and changing, we heard the results of the tournament—the This 'N That 4-H club had won the championship in the small club division. That was OUR club! We could not believe our ears, because we didn't think our scores were that good. But, sure enough, Mary and Amy went up to investigate and came back with five bronze medals in their hands. This was truly the icing on the cake. We came not knowing what to expect, and ended having such a fun time competing TOGETHER and having a great time the whole day. For those of you in 4-H, take a good look at this tournament for next year and come on out for a GREAT day of fun, TEAM SPIRIT, sportsmanship, and a chance to meet a lot of talented kids from nearby counties. We already plan to return next year…hope to see you there!

29

Renovating the Ranch

Every stable has its own special advantages and disadvantages. For example, the place where I board my horses, Kingsway Farm, in Winfield, has roomy stalls, plenty of pasture, daily turnout, is adjacent to DuPage County Forest Preserve trails, feeds quality feed, has a worming program, and gives a lot of TLC to all the animals. What more could you ask for, you ask?

That is exactly what Mr. Jim Joy, the barn's owner and manager, asked us, since he is always searching for ways to make improvements at Kingsway. The most popular request was for a good outdoor arena so we could practice our dressage and jumping in a standard sized arena. We weren't sure where he could fit one in on the property, but Mr. Joy knows his land!

One day we arrived at the barn to see part of the timber roped off in a very large rectangle, that would work out to a finished size of 120′ X 75′. Then he announced a "cutting" party for the next weekend. We were actually going to do this!

We arrived that next week with chain saw in hand and got down to business. It was hard to imagine our arena in this sea of brush and trees. We had a real "team" of workers. The men were the lumberjacks, cutting down the trees. We hauled twigs, sticks and logs into a big pile to be taken away. We had a lot of stumps left, and I wondered how in the heck we would get them out. Luckily, Mr. Joy found someone with a large bulldozer to come in and take them all out.

Each time we came out, there was more progress made. Finally, the "arena" was flat enough to ride in. I couldn't wait for the fence to be put up; I had to try it. It sure felt good to be able to work the horses in a large, flat arena with plenty of room.

In a few days, Mr. Joy put the fence up and it looked really nice. I was impressed. A few weeks later, my friends and I played Tom Sawyer and painted the fence white. Everyone always comments on how professional it looks. I think the best part about it is that since it is built in the woods, the big oak trees make a canopy over it, therefore making it shady and cooler in the heat. My horses love it! (and we humans appreciate it too!)

As if this were not enough, while the arena was being built, we were also working on jump standards so we could get our horses used to seeing stadium jumps. After Mr. Joy finished building five sets, my friend and I painted them white. He had the jump cups on order, and quickly we were decorating the interior of "our" ring.

So, what else is happening, you ask? Well, there is still some timber out there waiting for Mr. Joy to use his creativity in making a Cross Country course for us. And the best part about all of this is that we all have a chance to contribute our ideas, help, and be a part of the Kingsway family. And when new people come to the barn, we all take pride in knowing that "WE" did it...with a LOT of help from the Joys!

Mary Ruth and Amy show off their handiwork in the new arena

Torey

30

An Equispecial Trainer: Back to Basics

Although I have been riding for the past five years, sometimes I feel I should get back to basics for a while and brush up on the foundations of good horsemanship. So, I asked my trainer, Kathy Kelly, about the most common problems that occur in beginning riders, and what can be done to correct them.

The most common and biggest problem is that not enough emphasis is placed on the lower leg and heels. She says riders have to learn to keep their heels down and their legs tight and secure on the horse.

They also have to learn to develop a new kind of balance when riding a horse. Instead of using toes to balance, they have to use their leg and heel. "Most students seem to find their own balance, instead of the CORRECT balance," Kathy said. But she also says it's very hard to perfect your balance, and it takes a lot of work and time. I know this wasn't easy for me,

Kiki Osbourne

especially because I had to learn on my first horse, a BIG, young, Thoroughbred mare.

Kathy realizes that "Equitation is more than looking pretty...in addition you have to be effective." Kathy won't let her students progress until their leg position is secure. I found this out at my first lesson with her. She told me my legs weren't steady enough, and my weight wasn't in my heels, so she shortened my stirrups to "jockey" length and taught me my lesson with short stirrups. Wow! It sure made me put my heels down and think about my leg more. Otherwise, I would have found myself on the ground rather quickly!

The best ways to help solve these problems are to constantly work in a two-point (balanced position a rider is in over a jump) to learn balance at the walk, trot and canter, ride without stirrups with the correct leg position, or to longe the horse and rider together without stirrups or reins.

The next most common problem that Kathy sees is that beginning riders tend to pay attention to all the technical stuff like diagonals (while you are "posting", moving your body up and down, you must be up while the outside foreleg is moving forward) and leads and to not direct their attention to their basics. This surprises me because in the show ring many beginners seem not to worry about their horse. She said they need to look up and pay attention to their riding skills, not the horse.

Moving forward too quickly. Mmmmm...does that ring a bell? Has anyone ever told you that you should go back a step because you're pushing yourself

124

too much? I know I've heard that myself a number of times. Kathy said most everyone who rides wants to progress too quickly. They need to stop and take time on BASICS. (There's that word again!) Many riders think, "once they can walk, then they can trot, and when they trot, they can canter…Not true," says Kathy Kelly. Things should be mastered before moving on.

We all want our horses to look as good as they can when we ride them right? I know I do. I love my horse to look good. Unfortunately, that doesn't always happen. When riders don't know what they are doing, they can't make the horse do anything. Kathy would rather see riders ride well than have the horse look good.

So how does Kathy Kelly know all of this? She started riding at age 13 and was 16 when she got her first horse. She joined the Pony Club at 16 and worked for four years to get her "A" (the highest you can go in Pony Club!) at age 20. She started out eventing her horse and progressed to the Intermediate level. After eventing for a while, she decided she needed help with stadium jumping and worked with hunter people.

After several years, she had an opportunity to ride upper level dressage horses and achieved success at those levels. She liked it so much that she continued dressage for three years. A neat thing about Kathy is her versatility and the fact that she really loves all styles of riding. She is now training her own horse, Corey, to be a hunter.

Kathy teaches many students at all levels, including combined training (a three phase competition which includes dressage, cross country and stadium jumping) in the form of lessons and clinics. In addition to lessons, she judges dressage and does pony club ratings. Even among all of these activities, she still doesn't let us forget that one word: BASICS!

31

Equispecial Hunter Trials

Last weekend, early in the morning, with the weather well below 30 degrees, I shivered my way out to St. James Farm with my fuzzy horse, Cactus, to participate in a very unique, yet fun and exciting event—The St. James Chicagoland Hunter Trials. The trials are designed for people in the hunt to compete in a show. I was to find out that it was all a lot of friendly competition between members of area hunts. I was so excited because, as a Pony Club member, I was invited to participate.

The day before the trials I still hadn't decided for sure whether or not I was going because I knew it was going to be a frigid day. The forecast was for a sunny day, so I decided to try to brace the cold. That decision made, I read over the entry form and wondered what I was getting into. The requirements for ladies were "dark coat with hunt buttons and hunt colors on collar, buff or canary breeches, hunting bowler or approved headgear with harness secured. Long hair should be tied up and netted." Huh? That,

127

I found out, was for those members who had earned their "colors" in the hunt. As a Pony Clubber, I wouldn't have to worry about that—we were not expected to have the proper hunt attire, since we were "guests" at this competition.

So, at 6:45 a.m., we hooked up and headed out to St. James. When we got there I stepped out of the car and froze. How could I go through with this? I saddled up and went out to warm up and school over the fences. Fuzzy Cactus trotted around probably thinking, "This girl must be out of her mind." The jumps were only about 2'9", and the only bad one would be "the bank." We were ready!

We had time to watch other classes before we were "on." I watched about a dozen or so rounds of the older hunt members. They and their horses looked like pros rounding the course at a steady pace. I wondered how the judges could judge a class like this—they all looked so good.

Finally, it was time for our first class, a pony club field hunter class which is judged on how suitable your horse looks for hunting. I managed to get all my show clothes on, along with my winter jacket on top if it, and three pairs of gloves. Was I dressed properly?? Not to worry, I guess...Cactus "did his stuff" and stayed steady and honest enough to earn us first place.

We put our horses in the trailer to keep warm and found a warm tent to sit down in and watch some more classes. This was a tent hosted by members of the hunt, and they were very kind to let us share their warmth and refreshments.

After a morning of competition, we were treated to a really unusual form of entertainment during lunchtime. Terrier Races! Some people brought their little terriers, and other brought "non-terriers." A straight course was set up with little rows of jumps all the way to the finish line. I wasn't sure how they planned to make these dogs run over the fences, but I soon found out. They loaded the dogs into separate kennels and showed them a fox tail. By that time some turned around, and others were barking at it. The fox tail was tied at the end of a rope that someone hand-reeled up very fast while the dogs chased it. When the kennel doors opened up, the dogs were off. Well...some were off. A few ran for the tail and jumped the fences; some stood in one spot; some ran back through openings at the starting line; some decided to follow other dogs; and some searched for their owners. What fun! I'm considering taking my dog (a German Shepherd!) next year in the over 12" class, if he promises not to eat the competition.

After lunch we got back to the final classes of the day. One of our pony club classes was unique. Instead of riding by ourselves, we rode on a team of three people. Here was our chance to put to practical use one of the pony club's mottos of "teamwork." The key was to stay evenly spaced behind the lead horse — which looks much easier than it really is! We had to combine two, very long lanky Thoroughbreds with short, stout Cactus. The neatest part of the course was the last fence, where we were to end up lined up side by side and jump together. This was very unique, as we are not usually allowed to jump close to another horse. The best team we saw was a team of two white ponies and a paint horse. What a colorful sight they made moving across the hunt field, topped off with a wonderfully synchronized jump at the end!

There were several aspects to this competition that were different from others I have attended. First of all, there was a feeling of camaraderie between competitors. Then there were the trophies…what a sight! I have never seen so many perpetual trophies (prize given to someone one year, then passed along to the winner the next year) on one table before! I, of course, didn't miss checking out the Davies Cup that was to be awarded to the Championship Pony Club rider! One of my friends at our St. James Pony Club had won it last year, so I was hoping that someone from our club would win it again this year. (Me, perhaps?)

Finally, there was a different style of dress that was mandated for hunt members. It was all very colorful and interesting. For instance, there was something called the "Corinthian Working hunter," which was ridden in Hunt livery with emphasis placed on "brilliance of performance." Also considered was the equipment, which included some very different items such as sandwich cases, flasks, and wire cutters. This is something one does not see at your everyday hunt show or event.

During the day, not only did I have a great time competing, but I also had the opportunity to meet many new and nice people who belong to the Wayne-DuPage and other Hunts. I never realized there was such an interest in hunting right in this area. All of them were very supportive and helpful. I hope that we will see more people at next year's trials — it's great entertainment for all!

Now that I've tried the trials, I guess it's on to the hunt!

Kiki Osbourne

"The Final Jump" (I'm the one in the middle)

The Fourth Year

Mason demonstrates his jumping form to the other "horses."

Chrissy and I clear the oxer with ease

32

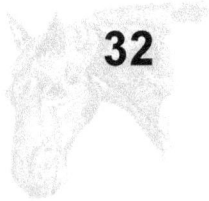

The Horseless Horse Show

"I believe that we all gained a better understanding of what our horses physically go through…"

About a month ago, my pony club had a unique Christmas party. I addition to all the annual activities, like a pot luck and a gift exchange, we held a Horseless Horse Show for all of us riders. You're probably wondering what this is exactly. I wondered about it myself before it took place. From what we had heard, we were supposed to act like horses in a show ring. How strange!

So on the night of the show, we "horses" arrived at the huge St. James indoor arena to find a table full of horse show ribbons and a bustle of happy, ready-to-go pony clubbers. We talked about what events we wanted to "compete" in. There were two dressage and two jumping classes planned. Most of us did every one we could. After we decided on the classes, we registered and got our numbers. Some kids stood around talking while others "schooled" over fences and tried out their "horse actions." We even had a "tack" inspection by Mr. John Davies, equestrian director at the farm.

The first class was hunter over fences. We walked the course with our coach, Mr. Davies. It was made up of many cavalettis (elevated rails used to teach a horse balance, rhythm and other skills) that didn't get higher than 18". Sounds pretty easy, huh? For horses, yes. For humans, it remained to be seen. It looked fun to me. A few people took their turn and finally it was mine. I did my courtesy circle and started the course. I made it clear and with what I thought was a good hunter pace. After my round, I found that it WAS hard work cantering around a course of cavalettis.

I left the ring breathing hard and feeling very tired. So I sat down to watch the other people go. There were many clear rounds but also some refusals. A few crazy "horses" acted up and ran around and crawled under the jumps. Finally they announced the winners of our class. There was tie for first place, so we even did the usual timed jump off.

Next, we all did a training level dressage test. This was even more tiring than the jumping class. After my ride, I found out that it takes a lot of energy to do one little dressage test. Poor horses! This event took quite a while because each test took about four minutes. The judge probably thought I lacked "impulsion" because I was getting so tired.

The last class was a pairs jumping class. My partner was my friend's younger sister. She and I were a great team. We did flying lead changes together and kept everything in synch. In this class they added an oxer (a jump with some width). It was much harder to get over than the normal jumps. Just think when horses have to jump over those four to five foot spreads. Wow!

I believe that we all gained a better understanding of what our horses physically go through when we compete. This is a wonderful way to brush up on dressage tests as well. So, who needs horses for a horse show? Give yours a rest and give it a try yourselves!

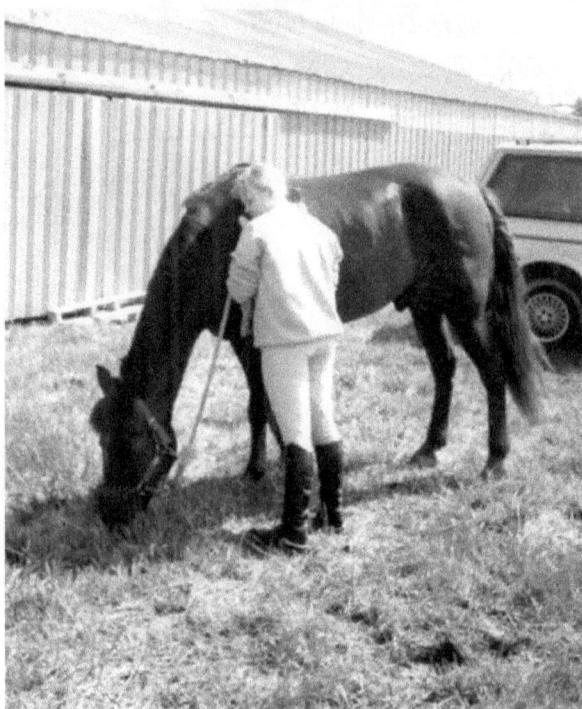

"Listen to me, Cactus."

33

An Open Letter to Cactus

We all thought it was a great idea to share board my horse, Cactus, with two new young riders in our pony club. After all, he was gentle, kind, just the right size, and old enough to "know the ropes" (17) yet snazzy enough to still pull off some very awesome performances. Perfect. The setup was supposed to help everyone—Cactus could take it easy because the girls would not work him very hard over the winter, they could work on their riding skills without worrying about a crazy horse, AND, I could still ride him whenever I wanted.

Cactus, however, has had some other ideas about this arrangement, and has been telling the girls about them in a very "un-Cactus-like" way, for example, *bucking*. I think it is important for us to let our horses know that some things are just not acceptable. On the other hand, we need to let them know when they are doing a good job. If any of you at Hobson Road stables are reading this month's Equine Market, please show this to Cactus.

I think he might like it.

Dear Cactus:

What's wrong? What don't you like about your new friends who absolutely love you and take such good care of you. I've never seen you buck to be mean, especially when you don't know who's on your back. I always thought you WANTED to carry your riders safely through a workout or trail ride, but maybe I'm wrong.

Torey and Morgan want to learn from you because you're such a good teacher. I learned almost everything about riding from you. You were so kind and gentle with me. If I was wrong, you never reprimanded me, but told me in your own subtle ways. Why can't Torey and Morgan learn the same unique way I did?

"Caci," you have so much talent. I know you want to do more, but please take your well-earned winter rest with a good attitude and be a gentleman to the girls. Save your bucks for the pasture, and if you want, me—I don't mind. You're still my number one horse and I'll NEVER sell you.

Unfortunately, I've been talked into training your friend Outryder for the winter, so I can't see you as much. This summer Outryder won't be close to your talents yet, so if you'd want to, and let me, I'd like to do some Novice eventing this year with you as my noble steed. Think you could handle it? I KNOW you can, and you'll have fun, too. But, you have to promise you'll act gentlemanly to your new friends and don't give them trouble. I look at pictures of you and am amazed you still look so wonderful, capable and kind.

Go for the first place in dressage rally with Morgan and Torey. Then, turn around the next day and fly like the wind over show-jumping fences for me. I know you can do it, you have the heart. I'll make more of an effort to come see you everyday and bring you your beloved carrots and peppermints. Please don't let my trust in you down!

Love,
Kiki

P.S. I miss you!

Cactus and me, ready for any show

34

Getting Ready for an Equispecial Season

It's showtime! Are you ready? The other day I started to think about what I needed to get ready for the fast-approaching "season," and was overwhelmed at all the details involved. After talking to my parents about my plans, I found out that it all boils down to one thing—budget. This refers to both time and money. I'd like to let you know about some of the things I considered, and how I organized everything, so that you can approach your parents with a little more "ammunition" than I did!

The first thing I attempted to do was pencil-in the dates of the shows and events I wanted to attend this summer. That wasn't easy, with other items already taking up space on my calendar. Nevertheless, I did manage to squeeze in a few events.

Next, I looked up every event in my USCTA (United States Combined Training Association) omnibus (book that lists information about all events) to find out entry fees and stabling costs. Each event was different in price — some were more expensive than others, and some were just too far away to consider. Then, I checked all of my old horse newsletters (like Pony Club, 4-H, etc.) and show bills to see if there were any mini-events or open shows I would like to attend. After looking at all of the prices of these, I was forced to eliminate some. NO FAIR! I wish I could do everything!

Then, I got down to the details. Would I have to pay stabling costs? If I rode Cactus all summer, I wouldn't have to worry about stabling costs, because he stands tied to a trailer without putting up a fuss. But, hopefully, I will be riding a new horse, and there is no guarantee that he will be as well behaved as Cactus. If I have to pay for a stall, it can be very expensive.

Speaking of the trailer — my family doesn't own a trailer, so we have to pay someone to trailer our horse. I found out that it can get very expensive if you need a ride almost every week-end.

Before you can go to an event or show, you must make sure that your horse is in good condition. The vet and farrier bills also take a chunk of the money. I like to have my horse checked over by the vet just to make sure he stayed sound over the winter. I make sure to have all of his shots up-to-date if I plan on taking him to other barns. Also, if you plan to go out-of-state, you must have proof of a Coggins test (a test for Equine Infectious Anemia, or Swamp fever) within the last year. In addition, you need a health certificate from your vet no more than 10 days before the trip.

Usually Cactus goes barefoot during the winter months, so I have to have his "Air Jordans" put on. ($$$!)

I took inventory of my horse's "clothes." WOW! There were a few questions I had to ask myself about my tack. Are my saddles and bridles well cleaned and oiled? Is the stitching safe? Do I have all the splint and bell boots my horse needs? Does my horse have sheets, blankets, and wraps for traveling? In general, do I need to have any tack repaired?

Then, there were those incidentals. If you board your horse, you probably don't think about extra water/feed buckets, muck bucket, shovel, manure fork, broom, and other cleaning tools. You must also have an equine first aid kit as well. I've recently added a horse stethoscope and thermometer that Santa delivered to me last Christmas.

O.K. Now I have my entry fees and horse taken care of; I'm ready, right? WRONG. I needed to make sure I had all of my own clothing in place. I tried on coats, breeches, and shirts, and I was pleasantly surprised that all of my breeches were very loose this year. Actually, that wasn't good at all! It means I'll have to go shopping for new breeches and spend money I could have used for entry fees. Darn! Here we go again with that "B" word—BUDGET.

My mom and I decided that the only way we could get a handle on all of these costs would be to make a chart that outlined all of the costs involved, and see where we stand—do we eliminate some events...can we add any? (Fat chance!) Here is what we came up with, as guidelines for keeping track of where you want to go, how much you might spend, and what you need. We arranged events according to date, and tried to include the most common expenses.

We now have a pretty good idea of what we can do this season, and we can plan ahead for trailering, etc. So, make your chart, add up expenses, and talk with your parents about it. Hopefully, you will be successful in your presentation, and then...I'll see you at the shows!

SAMPLE SHOW EXPENSE CHART:

Date	Event	Entry Fee	Stabl	Trail-er	Food	Other	Total
4/24	Pony Club Clinic	$15	$10	15			$40
5/1	Schooling Show	$50	$10	$20	$15		$95
5/29	Combined Test	$45	$15	$20	$15		$95
6/5	Pony Club Know Down Rally	$75			$15	$100 Hotel	$190
6/15	Fun Day	$25	$10	0	$10		$45
7/2	Mini Event	$40	$15	$20	$15		$90
7/16	Pony Club Dressage Rally	$65	$25	$50	$35	$100 Hotel	$215
7/23	Schooling Show	$50	$10	$20	$15		$95
8/11	Pony Club Clinic	$15	$10	$15			$40
8/16	Pony Club Combined Training Rally	$75	$25	$20	$35	$100 Hotel	$255
9/17	Horse Trials	$80	$30	$50	$40	$150 Hotel	$350
Total For Season							$1510

Kiki Osbourne

SHOW CHECKLIST

Horse::
Saddle
Bridle (jump/dressage)
Girth
Saddle pads
(schooling/show)
Jumping boots for horse
Breastplate/martingale
Brushes
Braiding kit (scissors,
clip, seam ripper, comb,
yarn, latch hook)
Show sheen
Hoof oil
Rags
Stud kit
Saddle stand
Bridle hook
Cleaning hook (to hang
tack while cleaning)
Tack cleaning supplies
Horse/human First Aid
Kit
Wraps
Liniment
Anti-sweat sheet
Wool cooler
Extra halter/lead rope
Bucket heater Buckets —
2 (water & feed)
Chains

Snaps
Bedding
Wheelbarrow
Pitchfork
Broom
Hay bag with hay
Coggins Test

Human::
Show coat
Show shirt
Breeches
Boots
Stock tie/pin
Gloves
Helmet(s) (dressage,
cross country, show
jumping)
Spurs
Crop
Medical armband
Watch

_If more than a one day
show:_
Appropriate number of
bales of hay
Grain, bagged and
labeled
Supplements

35

Shows, Shows, and More Shows

When I talked about getting ready for the show season last month, you probably thought you knew everything you needed to know and were all ready. Well, There is one teeny tiny item to consider: in WHAT KIND of show are you going to compete?

It may surprise you to know how many options there are. The range from competitive trail riding to eventing gives us horse owners many options. I've participated in a variety of competitions in my years working with horses.

The first year I showed my horse, Brittany, I competed in open shows. Why did I do this? Well, I really had no idea that there were any other choices. All of the people at my barn did it, so I went along! These are shows that have classes for every style of riding in them. For example a typical showbill order would be: halter classes for all breeds, Western classes, English classes, and lastly, any jumping, games or extra classes. There are usually between 25 and 50 classes per show day. After each class, ribbons are awarded, and sometimes division champion or high point awards are presented as well. That first year I didn't accumulate a lot of ribbons, BUT, I had a lot of fun at those shows and I met a lot of nice, interesting people from all over. I still occasionally go to some local open shows to give my young horse experience, and I STILL have fun.

Actually it was at these open shows that we made the "Pony Club Connection" which led me to join Pony Club, which, in turn, introduced me to a new form of showing: eventing. At first, I didn't understand it. Why did we only get ONE ribbon if we showed the whole day? I wasn't sure I wanted to "take a step on the wild side" and give up my open shows for this new stuff. I gave it a "test drive" a few summers ago and from then on decided to work on eventing. In eventing, you cover three phases: Dressage, Cross Country, and /stadium Jumping.

Traditionally, dressage comes first. It is important to have a good dressage test, as it sets the pace for the rest of the competition. If you are ahead after dressage and your horse can jump, you most likely will be "in the ribbons." Cactus and I do well in that first phase because he is such a steady horse. I found out that "steady" was the name of the game in dressage.

Cactus seemed to love cross-country. After he realized he was "free" nothing stopped him from cantering whole two foot course we were told to trot. I think both Cactus and I could have done the course three more times; we have so much fun! The final round is stadium. I think it is the hardest phase. I'm always worried I'll get eliminated in the last round. It hardly ever happens, but when it does it's usually my fault. At the end of the long, hot (but FUN, don't forget!) day, they announce the winners. Everyone who earns a placing gets to participate in a victory gallop around the stadium course. My horse loves to be in the gallop at the end of the day. (Okay, I do too!) I think he tries extra hard sometimes to be able to lead the gallop with a first place ribbon dangling from his bridle.

I've also competed in a version of competitive trail riding called the Hunter Pace. I like to do these; there is no pressure on you and your horse to perform well. We ride on a marked trail through forest preserves and sometimes even jumps are included. Usually a "head rider" rides the trail first and everyone else tries to come in close to their time.

There are also shows specializing in one specific breed such as Quarter Horse or Appaloosa. Most of these shows are held over the course of two or more days, but run on the same general basis of an open show. To participate in these types of shows, your horse must be registered as that particular breed.

In addition, there are shows for specific types of riding, such as saddleseat or hunter shows. Any breed of horse may be shown in these, but they must all be suitable for that style of riding. You can even go to an all dressage show, if you are interested in dressage only. You can stay local or go National. No matter where you are, you can find a show somewhere, every weekend that will fit your horse and style of riding. Take a chance, try something new.

Is your head spinning yet? You can find out about any of these shows through your barn, local equine publications, or the horse associations in your area. There are a lot of choices to be made, but once you decide and become a competitor, just remember, HAVE FUN, and you WILL be a winner!

Outryder

36

Grooming for Kathy

You might think that participating in an official event without a horse would be 1) not a lot of fun, and 2) easy. Wrong. Little did I know how much of the horse knowledge I have would be put to the test in the job of "Grooming for an Event."

Recently, my trainer Kathy Kelly, entered a novice event in Barrington, Illinois. Unfortunately, I was out of town the week before, so I was unable to prepare my own horse for competition as I'd hoped. I decided it would be just as much fun to spend the weekend in Barrington, grooming for Corey and Casey, the two horses Kathy was planning to ride.

When one of Kathy's mounts went lame (Corey), she called and asked if Outryder (my horse) might be available for her to use instead. I was so excited that my horse would have a novice event experience and that I was going to be learning the responsibilities of an event groom while working on my own horse.

Thursday night before the event I could hardly sleep. Friday morning arrived and I woke up very early so I could start my job. Since the day started off EARLY with dressage, our first entry, Outryder, had to be completely braided at least an hour before her test. I never knew how quickly I could braid a horse!

Soon I led my four-hooved masterpiece out of her stall, her ears up, ready to go. But, my job was just beginning. As Kathy mounted up and rode off to the warm-up area, I ran back to the tack area and grabbed a mane and tail comb, a rub rag, and Kathy's hunt coat. I couldn't forget my camera either. I then wiped all the extra dust off the horse and Kathy's riding boots. I also realized that someone (me) had to check the bit we were using to make sure it was a smooth snaffle.

While Kathy hopped off 'Ryder to put on her hunt coat, I took the horse to the bit check station (where a show official checks to see that your horse's bit is legal). On completion of the check, I led her back for Kathy to re-mount and finish her warm-up. I wiped off Kathy's boots and the horse one last time and wished them good luck. As both the groom and owner, I watched nervously as Ryder performed. After the test I led her back to her stall to take all of her tack off and cool her off. One horse down, one to go!

Casey was next up. I had two hours this time to get prepared, and by now I was experienced! I stood up on my little stepstool to braid his mane and he walked away. It took me five minutes to convince Casey that getting braids in his mane was not only fun, but it would make him look wonderful, too. This wasn't going to be easy, but he got used to it, gave up the fight, and I finished the job.

I found out that braiding two horses in one day really takes strong fingers! I tacked Casey up and repeated my "grooming" routine for a second time.

The day was over so quickly! However, this was the "Short" day. Tomorrow I faced FOUR preparations. Could I do it?

I got up early again on Saturday and headed to Barrington. This time, I thought, at least I won't have to braid. All I had to do was to "dress" the horses, so I started to put Outryder's splint and bell boots on her as soon as I arrived. Splint boots protect the horse's lower legs and the bell boots protect the horse's foot. She was saddled when Kathy arrived.

When I walked the mighty steed out, I gave the tack one last look to make sure everything was safe. Kathy mounted and rode off to the warm-up area with me following close behind, a cooler (a light, mesh blanket) and lead rope in hand. I arrived at the course a few minutes before start time, so I ran out to a fence and waited for them to gallop by. When they did, I dashed back to the finish line to take Outryder when Kathy dismounted. I loosened the girth and noseband and put a cooler on her so she wouldn't get chilled.

With the long walk back to the stable area Outryder was fairly cool by the time I got her back to the stall. I untacked her and went to the wash racks to sponge her off with the water I had pumped earlier that morning. I threw the cooler back on and I let her eat grass and take small sips of water until she was recovered enough to return to her stall.

By the time Outryder returned, it was time to get Casey ready for Cross Country. I booted and tacked him up the same way I did Outryder an hour earlier. Casey looked alert and ready to jump anything. The walk to the starting box was getting long and tiring. The second or third time I felt like my legs were going to fall off!

I was at the finish line to get a sweaty Casey. I put his cooler on him and we walked back to his stall. I untacked him and sponged him off till he was cool.

I was finding that there is a lot of walking involved in grooming. However, I had to keep my mind on my work. There was still one phase left: Stadium Jumping.

So, I saddled up 'Ryder for the SECOND time that day. I put the boots on her legs again, bridled her and led her out to Kathy. I jogged back to the barn just like the day before, grabbed a rag to wipe off the horse, Kathy's boots, and my camera.

A few horses before she had to ride, I gave Kathy her hunt coat and wished her luck. After a clear round, I took the horse as Kathy dismounted. I was so proud of Outryder! The whole way back I told her what a good girl she had been that day. When we arrived at the stalls, I untacked her and fed her tons of carrots and started getting the next mount ready.

As I tacked Casey for the final time, he seemed to be snoozing in his stall so I was a little worried he might fall asleep on the job. But he had different plans. After Kathy mounted Casey and took him over some warm-up fences, he suddenly came to life and cruised the course. As with Outryder earlier, I cooled off Casey and gave him carrots as I untacked him.

Both horses were going to need standing wraps for the night because of the hard work they'd done that day. So, I wrapped Ryder's legs after I rubbed her down with liniment and got her ready to be shipped home.

It seemed late in the day after all the hard work, but it was only early afternoon when we were ready to leave. Wow, how time doesn't fly when you're working! I would say that if you have never had a chance to be around a big event, volunteer your services. I've heard that good, experienced grooms even get paid for their expertise. Isn't it great that you can work and have FUN at the same time?

Shade Dancer shares his trailer with Cactus

37

An Equispecial Trailering Lesson

Cactus (Mr. Dependable, Mr. Cool) jumped, reared, whinnied, and absolutely refused to walk in the trailer. My dad was ready to shoot him. Mom had been waiting in the car for over an hour and a half, and my brother, Cody, just wanted to leave us both there overnight.

On a day I'll never forget, I got a real lesson on trailer-loading a horse. I was at my friend Alesia Hook's house, preparing myself and Cactus for a pony club rally. We planned to get up early, load all of our tack, load the horses at 9:00 and leave by 9:30. Cactus had a different plan.

As we prepared our horses for the long ride to Iowa, I thought Cactus was excited about going. But when I walked him up to the trailer, he stopped dead in his tracks and then proceeded to rear back. Immediately, we put a chain over his nose, and still no luck. Everyone tried to coax him in: Alesia's dad and mom, my dad and mom. Nothing worked.

We thought of the weirdest things, like pulling a tractor up to the side of the trailer. This was supposed to prevent him from moving sideways, but nothing would stop Cactus; he moved the other way. Having no luck with the tractor, we tried another bright idea.

I put Cactus back in his stall, and I'm sure at that point he was thinking he had won the trailering war. Little did he know that the trailer was making its way to him. Mr. Hook backed the opening of the trailer to Cactus's stall door. We wanted him to walk in by himself and we thought it might be more convincing if there was hay in the "Black Hole." No luck. He stood in the corner of his stall and made no effort to look at the trailer.

By this time, we had spent three hours trying to load the stubborn brat and we were running out of ideas. We moved the trailer outside and tried to load him again. This time we tried to convince him by wrapping a lunge line around his rump and pulling him in. Cactus stood there like a rock, not moving. The lunge line was thrown aside and we decided to try our last resort: a professional loader.

Everyone was so beat from this loading ordeal, we were willing to pay anything if they'd get Cactus loaded. When the pro showed up, she immediately put a chain over Cactus's nose and walked him to the trailer. She asked him to come forward and when he'd back up, she'd put pressure on the chain. If he did what she wanted him to, she applied no pressure. In addition, she had a new twist to the lunge line trick:

two of them cris-crossed, with a strong person at each end. Within fifteen minutes Cactus was loaded. I wondered if we would have to leave him in Iowa, once we got there! By now, maybe I wanted to!

After that experience, I've never had problems convincing Cactus to get in the trailer. It was difficult to believe that some horses take even longer to teach than Cactus.

For example, another trailering dilemma came up when my friend Torey called me and told me about her horse's recent loading problem. She'd bought a new trailer and tried to load Misty in order to take her to the vet. For nearly an hour, Torey, her dad, and a friend tried to coax Misty in. They used a lunge line and tried to feed her hay, but nothing worked. Finally, to everyone's surprise, Misty jumped in and no one knew why. Torey told me that when I came to visit, I'd have to help her train Misty to trailer load.

So, the next time I visited Torey, we got right to work. The first thing we did was to bring the trailer into the barn so we'd have a place to work all the time. Next, we tried to just normally walk her into the trailer. As Torey predicted, Misty reared back and refused. Immediately I put a lunge line behind her rump and tried to pull her in. It took us fifteen minutes until she finally jumped in. After Misty was in the trailer we fed her dinner and let her know it wasn't all that bad.

We thought back on how we actually coaxed Misty in and we concluded that because we kept her head straight and looking into the trailer, she felt more comfortable getting in. Twice a day we put Misty into the trailer to familiarize her. The first few times we had problems as she danced and reared around us, but she got better as the week went on. By the time I left, Misty walked right into the trailer with no hesitation.

Trailering doesn't have to be a terrible experience providing you spend some time training your horse to load. Personally, I believe that almost any horse can be trained to load and trailer calmly and safely. But one word of advice, don't try to "train" your horse to load the day of the big show!

38

Breeches and Burma Shave

As I looked back over my shoulder, I saw Mason and Joette, both covered head to toe with shaving cream, running toward me with foaming cans of Burma Shave in their hands. I knew I was destined to be their next victim.

Over the next 10 minutes, the entire crew took part in the biggest shaving cream fight in Pony Club history. As she squeezed the last ounce of shaving cream on my head, Joette turned to me and proclaimed, "I have more fun at Pony Club rallies than at anything else I ever do."

Later that evening, as I thought over the events of the last four days, I knew that she was right. Pony Club rallies should be a part of every young horse lover's tour of duty.

With that thought in mind, let me offer a mini tour of the North Central Regional C-Rally (at Barrington Hills this year) which I rode in last month.

Pony Club rallies are team competitions in which you're judged not only on how well you ride, but on

your horse and stable management abilities too. Each
year, separate regional rallies are held for and
Dressage, Show Jumping. "C" and "D" rallies are also
held each year. These are Combined Training rallies,
at the novice and training levels, and include the three
phases of Horse Trials: Dressage, Cross Country, and
Show Jumping.

Thursday afternoon we loaded our horses and set
off to begin our "C rally adventure." When we
arrived at Barrington Equestrian Center, Martha, our
premier stable manager, was setting up the tack room.
A typical rally team includes a stable manager along
with four riders, who all work together like a well-
oiled machine. Everyone helped to "decorate" the
tack stall with saddles, bridles and coat racks. After
"decorating" we arranged the rest of our equipment
properly.

Like the tack room, the horses' stalls had to be
made neat, clean, and safe, too. We removed or
covered protruding or sharp objects (nails, etc.) so the
horses wouldn't get hurt. Pony Club rules require
two buckets of water and a feed bin in every horse's
stall, so two buckets and a bin it was.

Each contestant was required to furnish a stall
card containing specific information including age,
breed, height, pulse, respiration, temperature,
veterinarian, farrier, special problems, and feed
schedule, for their horse. Each piece of information
had to be addressed or points would be deducted
from rally scores.

Finally, everything was in order and we dashed
off to our briefing. During the briefing, all of the team

members were introduced to the judges and officials and they explained how the rally was going to be run.

Our first major hurdle was a written test covering our equine knowledge (our horse sense), which included questions from veterinary facts to rally rules.

After the test, we returned to the stables where each horse was jogged in front of a vet to assure soundness for the next day's competition. We fed our horses and "tucked-em in" for the night. The first day of the rally was completed so we drove back to the hotel room to rest up for day 2...formal inspection and dressage.

Friday morning we were up early, preparing the horses for inspection. During the inspection, judges checked all tack, making sure it was not only spotless but SAFE (no rotten or broken stitching, etc.). They checked the horses thoroughly to make sure they were groomed properly. We were evaluated on the neatness of our formal and informal dress (i.e., black coat with stock tie or other colored coat with ratcatcher — informal neckwear for hunt attire) as well.

Exactly an hour after formal inspection, we performed our dressage tests. For me, that hour of warm-up passed so quickly. The next thing I knew, I was at point "X" saluting the judge. You don't waste time at a Pony Club Rally.

When I returned to the stable area, Martha was already getting other team members ready for their inspections. Within an hour after dressage, I proceeded to "turnback." I took my tack, my boots and my horse to a judge for inspection to make sure that all of the dirt was removed after riding. No stone is left unturned at a P.C. rallly.

We then took the official Cross Country tour with our coach. Each team is always required to have a coach for the jumping phases of the competition.

Finally we were done with day 2! Two down, 2 more to go! We did barn chores, and prepared for the next day's event, Cross Country!

Back at the hotel, we settled in for the evening with team members, chaperones, and other teams, too. You see, at Pony Club Rallies, the teams all stick together for the entire competition. Since our region includes a five-state area, we generally arrange for all the teams to stay at the same place. It is a great way to get to know other Pony Clubbers from all over the Midwest!

On the downside, we had to hit the pavement early enough to feed the horses. Once all the chores were done, we headed to the Cross Country area to do one more course walk.

We dropped off things like buckets, sponges, and people water, which we might need after completing the course. When we got back, I had to prepare quickly because I was scheduled to be the first rider on our team. Martha and I took Cactus out to brush him good and clean.

In Pony Club, protective boots are supposed to be taped on your horse so they won't fall off while he's galloping the course. It took 10 minutes just to tape on the boots. Then Martha finished tacking him up while I put on my safety vest—just in case—and because my mom would have a fit if I didn't wear it! (O.K., I admit, it's not too bad!) I got safety checked, mounted up and walked out to the course.

I found our coach at the warm-up area and rode over to the start box. As they counted down 10 seconds, I set my watch to measure my pace. I finished the course with only one refusal — not a great success, but not a failure either.

It's also a pony club rule that you ask permission before you dismount. This helps the organizers keep track of the competitors. Martha ran up my stirrups while I walked Cactus over to the vet box to have his pulse and respiration taken. Then I cooled him down and returned for a second check, receiving permission to return to the stable.

The last day of the rally began with another soundness jog. Before we started stadium, we participated in one of the most impressive parts of the rally — the Parade of Teams, which is comparable to the Parade of Nations in the Olympic Games. Everyone participated as a team, while each stable manager carried the team's banner. Preparing our horses for the parade was the most hectic part, because everyone has the same start time.

That final day began with dark clouds hanging ominously overhead. Sitting on Cactus in the pouring rain, I wondered how we would safely finish the course on the slippery grass. But realizing they would not stop the show, I began to ride.

I cleared jumps one thru seven, but just like last year's "D" rally, I almost forgot fence eight. I caught myself before it was too late and only picked up a couple penalty points instead of being eliminated.

Kiki Osbourne

Several of my teammates went thru the course clean or with minimal penalties.

Not long after the last rider had finished, naturally the rain let up. Nevertheless, we all gave it our best.

We came prepared to compete, and we returned home with more knowledge about pony club, teamwork, horses, and of course, shaving cream.

39

State Fair!

The best part of watching was noticing the array of fancy, colorful outfits the riders wore.

As the spoon in my mouth became unsteady, the egg rolled off and splattered on the ground. In the famous egg and spoon class, I saw the blue ribbon slipping away. It was the end of my first state 4-H horse show in Springfield.

I'd heard about this show numerous times, and finally, this year, I was able to compete. I thought, "What an opportunity for 4-Hers enrolled in the horse project; free stalls, free classes, competition at all age levels in all styles of riding—even driving!" It takes a lot of work, but with team effort, the chores didn't seem so bad and team support helped us through the competition.

The trip to Springfield took four long hours. Before we were able to put our horses in their stalls, we sprayed the stall walls and floors with Lysol disinfectant. After the horses were settled, our six-member team unloaded tack and organized the tack room with saddle and bridle racks. Later on, after the dirty work was completed, we took the horses out for a workout in the indoor arena. We couldn't wait to ride in the coliseum.

Early the next morning, the fairgrounds came to life with people everywhere getting ready to show. In the warm-up arena there were a ton of Western riders mixed in with Huntseat riders and even a few Saddleseat riders. The classes didn't start until one o'clock in the afternoon, so we had time to make Cactus's braids look great.

By noon, three of the DuPage County members, including Mary and Mary Ruth and I, were saddled and ready to school over the fences in the coliseum. Finally, at one o'clock, the first class (hunter over fences) started. Everyone from DuPage had clean rounds! Yes!!! During the rest of the day, there were more jumping classes and one flat class. We had a great time watching other riders in 4-H from around the state.

Early Thursday morning we rolled out of bed and rushed to the barn to start braiding for the scheduled dressage and hunter classes. This time, instead of seeing a ton of riders in the warm-up arena, there were hundreds of kids leading their spotless horses around in clean bridles waiting to compete in halter classes.

The call for dressage was at one o'clock. There were only a few riders waiting to show while I rode my test. I guess most of the riders showed up later because there were a lot of entries—almost fifty! The class continued throughout the rest of the day and into the evening. I'd never seen such a large dressage class in my whole life!

Later on, Kristen, Mary Ruth, and I competed in our "Hunter on the Flat" class. The class was extra large, and none of us made it into the ribbons, but we still had fun. We said, "Good Night" to the horses, fed them carrots and headed for a relaxing evening at the hotel.

Friday was an especially relaxing day for the English riders, so, we got to watch some of the show. Western pleasure and horsemanship took up most of our time. It was a lot of fun watching the Quarter Horses jog and lope so slowly around the ring. I didn't realize that a horse could actually move so slowly because none of the horses I ride have a slow gait.

The best part of watching was noticing the array of fancy, colorful outfits the riders wore. The sparkling shirts were such a contrast to the huntseat riders' conservative attire. Most of their saddles and bridles were covered with silver and were spotless. I've had a lot of people tell me English is fancy, but this made me think twice.

My mom decided we had to leave on Friday, so, much to my dismay, I had to pack everything up, say goodbye to everyone, including my horse, and we drove off into the sunset with the show still in progress and my mind still at the coliseum. Next year, I thought as we drove away, I'll glue that egg to my spoon. Think the judge will notice?

"Welcome, Gus"

40

Buying That Special Horse

I walked into Fox Meadow Farms early this morning to find my new black thoroughbred, Gus, waiting for me. For a year I have been wanting a new horse, and finally in June, I found Gus, the wonder horse. Since then, we've worked on figuring out how we could buy him. For the past three weeks we've been getting vet okays on him. This experience has made me realize how much goes into buying a new horse.

It all started when my trainer told me about this wonderful horse that was for sale in Springfield. First problem: far away! But, we also thought that there would be an advantage in knowing the people from whom we were buying. So, even before we had our other horse sold (second problem) we took a road trip to Springfield to "just take a look." (Strike three)

After three and a half hours of driving we finally arrived at Gus'ss house and rushed to his stall to find him eating his hay. We called his name, he looked up for a split second, then went back to eating. We decided to give him a chance anyway, and took him out, to check him out.

I checked him over from head to hoof according to Pony Club standards and did not find anything wrong with him. We checked out his legs very carefully, since I knew I wanted an event horse, and found them (the bones) to be quite clean for a 10 year old horse. His temperament was very calm and mild, something my mom thought was VERY important. After that, we saddled him so that I could ride him.

His owner got on first, so that I could see him move at the walk, trot, and canter, and also see what he was trained to do. His strong suit is dressage, and he looked great! When it was my turn, the owner gave me a lot of hints about which "button" to push when. He was different from my other horses that needed some "ho" (stop). He only needed some leg, but he was never out of control. I was sorry when it was time to put him away.

He was well behaved when we sponged him off and brushed him. I again checked over his legs and the rest of his body and STILL found no glaring problems. We took more time to talk with the owner and take a look at his papers, some photos and dressage scores. Quite an impressive picture.

On the way home it was hard to focus on the fact that we were there to "just take a look." I told my mom how much I would love to have Gus, and began to brainstorm how I could pay for him. I knew I had to sell my horse Outryder first, and I would also have to be sure and have a part-time job to pay for the upkeep of the new horse.

What I found out about buying and selling horses was that it appeared to be much easier to find a horse to buy, but not so easy to sell one. I had a hard time trying to understand it, because I know that I have a nice horse to sell also. So, now came the waiting. We said that we would absolutely not get another horse until I sold Outryder.

What I then found out was that NOTHING is absolute. We kept in touch with the owner of Gus and told her to let us know if there was any other interest, because we were really interested.

By late July nothing had changed. So, during my trip to the 4-H State Horse Show in Springfield I visited my dream horse. I wanted to make sure that he was still the horse I wanted. After being with him and riding him, I was sure. We decided to take the next step and make a deposit on him to "hold" him until we had time to sell our other horse.

We waited for a couple of weeks, then made a decision to go ahead with the final check out of the horse. He already had some X-rays taken at the beginning of the summer, and we were able to have two different vets evaluate them. Having X-rays enabled us to check for any unsoundnesses that were not visible, such as ringbone, sidebone or navicular which could possibly make a horse lame for the rest of his life.

After three weeks of musical X-rays, we had a vet exam done. What is interesting is that the vet can only give an opinion as to what he finds physically and on the X-rays, and it is up to the buyer to make an intelligent decision in the purchase of the horse. We based our decision on confidence in our vets as well as in the seller of the horse, who just happened to be a Pony Club family.

If I were to give you some hints on buying a horse, based upon my experience with Gus, I would say:

*Be patient. Your dream horse IS out there!

*Go back to see the horse several times.

*Always have a pre-purchase exam and, if possible, X-rays.

*Sell your old horse FIRST.

*Be patient.

Last Saturday night I couldn't sleep and I was up early Sunday, ready to greet Gus. It seemed FOREVER getting to the barn that morning. When I arrived at the barn, his old owner was standing by his stall giving him last minute tips, I'm sure. His new owner (hey, that's me!!) was ready to take over.

41

Pony Club, The Festival

Hundreds of horses and young riders assembled in the infield of the track to take part in the opening ceremonies of the 1992 United States Pony Club Festival (held August 5-8). A group of unmounted participants gathered together behind the horses. Over the loudspeaker, the announcer named every region to which the participating clubs belong. Immediately after, the American, Canadian, and British national anthems were played. Everyone started to clap and scream...Festival had officially begun!

For those of you who don't know what Festival is...It is a Pony Club event that happens only once every three years. It is the Ultimate Pony Club Meeting of members (mounted and unmounted) from all over the country and beyond. It lasts three-and-a-half days and is jam-packed with educational horse activities from morning to night! The site is, most appropriately, the Kentucky Horse Park in Lexington, Kentucky. Our North Central Region was well represented with clubs from Wayne Dupage, St. James, North Star, Sangamon Valley, Fox River Valley, Heart of Illinois. Most members from our club attended this event without horses, and I discovered that clinics can still be fun and interesting not viewed from my horse's back.

Early the first morning the unmounted and mounted pony clubbers gathered in the covered arena for information about the next few days of clinics. We were divided into groups of about eight kids, but the worst part about it was that no one knew each other. After meeting my mystery group, though, I realized that I was having tons of fun meeting new friends from all over the country.

One of my new friends lives in California, one in Florida, and another one in Massachusetts. There was even someone from the Virgin Islands! Wow! They sure did come from all over! Our group quietly huddled together as we waited for our group leader (who happened to be a pony club mom) to take us to the morning clinics, a conformation and veterinary clinic.

Our leader arrived and herded us out into the fresh Pony Club Festival air. The conformation class was held in the barn area so they could use a horse to demonstrate. Older "A" pony clubbers ran this clinic. They evaluated and compared two or three different horses' conformation strengths and weaknesses.

I enjoyed having the opportunity to critique real live horses who didn't have picture-perfect conformation. I liked seeing horses with conformation flaws I'd never seen before, so I could identify them.

Everyone watching the clinic was involved in answering different questions from, "What is the ideal slope for a shoulder?" to "Is this horse's overall conformation good?"

During our discussion with the vet, we learned to identify many different diseases that we find in our equines around the U.S., what results from them, and if there any preventative vaccines available. Almost everyone in the group got to share personal experiences with sickness and their horses. We all enjoyed hearing normal, everyday horse people tell their stories.

Throughout the rest of the afternoon we attended more clinics, the Kentucky Horse Park Parade of Breeds, and Polo-crosse. They apparently planned for us to work in the morning and have our fun in the afternoon. After eating our sack lunches, we kicked back and watched the Parade of Breeds. Some of the breeds represented were Berkshire Curly Hair, Friesian, Haflinger, and even a miniature horse!

Each horse did a little routine to music (with the help of a rider, of course!) and, at the very end, all of the animals finished back in the ring together. Even though this does not sound highly educational, it actually helped some of us to recognize certain breeds of horses.

Then we all stampeded over to a Polo-crosse clinic. I was very anxious to learn how to play a new sport that I know nothing about. First off, I was handed a racquet, or a mallet, or whatever it was. It was a long stick with a little circular net at the end. Basically, it was a cross between a polo stick and a Lacrosse stick.

For a whole hour we paired up to practice throwing and catching the balls. My partner and I had a lot of trouble at first, especially with getting the ball to come out of the net. Catching turned out to be the easier part. Throughout our lesson there were two or three little boys who played Polo-crosse helping us. Even though I finally got the hang of throwing and catching, I felt like a fool with these "experts" always keeping a close watch on us.

The head coach told us a few basic rules of the game so we could watch the game that night and understand it. I couldn't wait to see these kids coordinate riding a horse and throwing a polocrosse ball at the same time in an exhibition game. That first evening was spent at the Horse Park watching teams from all over playing the game.

Bright and early the next morning the same herd of pony clubbers showed up to the Horse Park for a second day of Festival. Surprisingly, I found everyone from my group wide awake and ready for a rousing discussion on equine first-aid. A vet answered many, many questions people wanted to ask pertaining to first aid.

After our discussion, some of my friends attended more clinics on nutrition, fox hunting and driving, while others of us toured the Kentucky Horse Park. We visited the horse museum for an hour or so. It was fun and interesting to learn the history of our four-hooved friends. I enjoyed reading about famous horses and their accomplishments the most.

We walked back to the covered arena and decided to try a vaulting clinic. Unfortunately, we had time only to vault once because there were so many people who wanted to try to jump on a horse bareback. Surprisingly enough, I was able to jump on the trotting horse without any help. I wished we had more time to practice so I could learn more about the riding part of vaulting.

The strangest thing about vaulting is that it requires no hard hats. Usually, Pony Club always enforces the rule, but I guess it's easier to do tricks without a big, bulky helmet. I felt a little unsure riding with nothing on my head. A lot of St. James members decided they really enjoyed vaulting, so hopefully, we're going to start to vault in our Pony Club.

That evening we were drawn back to the Horse Park for something called the "Haagen Dazs Shuffle." This was an amazing combination of entertainment and all the ice cream you could eat. Kids teamed up to take a turn at the Karaoke singing machine for some "non-horsey" horsin' around. They showed us they had more than horse talent!

Then, the last day of festival had arrived. We had only three clinics scheduled that afternoon: bandaging, trailering, and longeing.

At the bandaging clinic, the leader demonstrated the correct way to wrap a shipping, a standing and an exercise wrap, and then made us practice on each other's legs. What a weird feeling-having your leg wrapped.

The longeing demonstration was in the covered arena. There weren't any horses available to longe, so we did something a little odd, like bandaging our own legs and lunging each other. Every "horse" cooperated quite nicely as we learned the different stages used to teach a horse to longe. I wish all of our horses were so well behaved as these.

There was SO MUCH to see and do at Festival, both mounted and unmounted, it was impossible to "do it all." From clinics to foxhunting to scavenger hunts to terrier races, even. This truly was an extraordinary event. The number of people involved was staggering: There were 2,191 Pony Clubbers attending. Special seminars were attended by 1,295 parents and friends. There were 150 riders in the Foxhunt! And most importantly, it took a staff of 606 VOLUNTEERS to make this all happen.

After the last clinic ended, all of my new friends and I hung around and talked about our Festival experiences. As I exchanged addresses and phone numbers with one of my friends from California, I thought back to four days ago. The opening ceremonies had just begun, and I wondered how in the world I was going to meet all of these people. But I soon realized that it was easy to make friends if they had one thing in common: Pony Club. I know I'll be ready in three years, mounted or not, for the NEXT Pony club Festival!

The Fifth Year

Brittany and me…ready to sing our Christmas duet

42

The Twelve Days of Christmas: Two Equispecial Versions

During the Christmas season I often find myself humming a carol or two. So, I've decided to write a song for you and your horse to sing at Christmastime. Now you can sit back, relax, and enjoy the Twelve Horsey Days of Christmas!

FOR YOU:

On the First Day of Christmas my good friend gave to me a Big Black Gelding Named Gus.

On the Second Day of Christmas my good friend gave to me Two riding boots and A Big Black Gelding Named Gus.

On the Third Day of Christmas my good friend gave to me Three Leather Halters, Two riding boots and A Big Black Gelding Named Gus.

On the Fourth Day of Christmas my good friend gave to me Four Matching Splint Boots, Three Leather Halters, Two riding boots and A Big Black Gelding Named Gus.

On the Fifth Day of Christmas my good friend gave to me FIVE PAIRS OF CHAPS, Four Matching Splint Boots, Three Leather Halters, Two riding boots and A Big Black Gelding Named Gus.

On the Sixth Day of Christmas my good friend gave to me Six Approved Hard Hats, FIVE PAIRS OF CHAPS, Four Matching Splint Boots, Three Leather Halters, Two riding boots and A Big Black Gelding Named Gus.

On the Seventh Day of Christmas my good friend gave to me Seven Prepaid Entries, Six Approved Hard Hats, FIVE PAIRS OF CHAPS, Four Matching Splint Boots, Three Leather Halters, Two riding boots and A Big Black Gelding Named Gus.

On the Eighth Day of Christmas my good friend gave to me Eight Polo Wraps, Seven Prepaid Entries, Six Approved Hard Hats, FIVE PAIRS OF CHAPS, Four Matching Splint Boots, Three Leather Halters, Two riding boots and A Big Black Gelding Named Gus.

On the Ninth Day of Christmas my good friend gave to me Nine Turnout Rugs, Eight Polo Wraps, Seven

Prepaid Entries, Six Approved Hard Hats, FIVE PAIRS OF CHAPS, Four Matching Splint Boots, Three Leather Halters, Two riding boots and A Big Black Gelding Named Gus.

On the Tenth Day of Christmas my good friend gave to me Ten Leather Girths, Nine Turnout Rugs, Eight Polo Wraps, Seven Prepaid Entries, Six Approved Hard Hats, FIVE PAIRS OF CHAPS, Four Matching Splint Boots, Three Leather Halters, Two riding boots and A Big Black Gelding Named Gus.

On the Eleventh Day of Christmas my good friend gave to me Eleven Pairs of Breeches, Ten Leather Girths, Nine Turnout Rugs, Eight Polo Wraps, Seven Prepaid Entries, Six Approved Hard Hats, FIVE PAIRS OF CHAPS, Four Matching Splint Boots, Three Leather Halters, Two riding boots and A Big Black Gelding Named Gus.

On the Twelfth Day of Christmas my good friend gave to me Twelve Pairs of Bell Boots, Eleven Pairs of Breeches, Ten Leather Girths, Nine Turnout Rugs, Eight Polo Wraps, Seven Prepaid Entries, Six Approved Hard Hats, FIVE PAIRS OF CHAPS, Four Matching Splint Boots, Three Leather Halters, Two riding boots and A Big Black Gelding Named Gus

Kiki Osbourne

FOR YOUR HORSE:

On the First Day of Christmas my owner gave to me A Big Pasture Filled with Green Grass.

On the Second Day of Christmas my owner gave to me Two cups of Bran Mash, and A Big Pasture Filled with Green Grass.

On the Third Day of Christmas my owner gave to me Three Huge Apples, Two cups of Bran Mash, and A Big Pasture Filled with Green Grass.

On the Fourth Day of Christmas my owner gave to me Four New Shoes, Three Huge Apples, Two cups of Bran Mash, and A Big Pasture Filled with Green Grass.

On the Fifth Day of Christmas my owner gave to me FIVE STRAW FILLED STALLS, Four New Shoes, Three Huge Apples, Two cups of Bran Mash, and A Big Pasture Filled with Green Grass.

On the Sixth Day of Christmas my owner gave to me Six Sugar Cubes, FIVE STRAW FILLED STALLS, Four New Shoes, Three Huge Apples, Two cups of Bran Mash, and A Big Pasture Filled with Green Grass.

On the Seventh Day of Christmas my owner gave to me Seven Water Buckets, Six Sugar Cubes, FIVE STRAW FILLED STALLS, Four New Shoes, Three

Huge Apples, Two cups of Bran Mash, and A Big Pasture Filled with Green Grass.

On the Eighth Day of Christmas my owner gave to me Eight Peppermints, Seven Water Buckets, Six Sugar Cubes, FIVE STRAW FILLED STALLS, Four New Shoes, Three Huge Apples, Two cups of Bran Mash, and A Big Pasture Filled with Green Grass.

On the Ninth Day of Christmas my owner gave to me Nine Bales of Hay, Eight Peppermints, Seven Water Buckets, Six Sugar Cubes, FIVE STRAW FILLED STALLS, Four New Shoes, Three Huge Apples, Two cups of Bran Mash, and A Big Pasture Filled with Green Grass.

On the Tenth Day of Christmas my owner gave to me Ten Hooved Friends, Nine Bales of Hay, Eight Peppermints, Seven Water Buckets, Six Sugar Cubes, FIVE STRAW FILLED STALLS, Four New Shoes, Three Huge Apples, Two cups of Bran Mash, and A Big Pasture Filled with Green Grass.

On the Eleventh Day of Christmas my owner gave to me Eleven Pounds of Carrots, Ten Hooved Friends, Nine Bales of Hay, Eight Peppermints, Seven Water Buckets, Six Sugar Cubes, FIVE STRAW FILLED STALLS, Four New Shoes, Three Huge Apples, Two cups of Bran Mash, and A Big Pasture Filled with Green Grass.

On the Twelfth Day of Christmas my owner gave to me Twelve Bags of Sweet Feed, Eleven Pounds of Carrots, Ten Hooved Friends, Nine Bales of Hay, Eight Peppermints, Seven Water Buckets, Six Sugar Cubes, FIVE STRAW FILLED STALLS, Four New Shoes, Three Huge Apples, Two cups of Bran Mash, and A Big Pasture Filled with Green Grass.

Now that you and your horse have caught on, don't be surprised to hear the whole barn caroling the holidays away!

Everybody sing...and...MERRY CHRISTMAS!!

43

10 Checkpoints for Choosing a Home for Your Horse

Three weeks ago, several of my friends and I went on a barn tour in suburban Chicago. Before I went, I listed 10 checkpoints according to which I planned to rate each of these barns. And if I were choosing a barn for Cactus (my favorite horse) today, I would do it according to the following criteria.

First I checked for stall cleanliness. I certainly don't want my horse Cactus to live in a dump. Clean stalls mean that the odds of a horse getting worms, thrush, colic, etc. are reduced greatly. So I feel it is important that stalls are cleaned daily!

Not only did I check for stall cleanliness, but I also checked the people's places too...such as the tack room, the office, and the lounge. I don't want my saddles and bridles in a dusty moist room where the leather could be ruined. Tack should be kept in a nice, dry, clean area, so this part is important too.

Next, I want to ride in a good place. Trails are fun, but I want an area where I can school, too. I've seen stables with rings as small as dog pens. I've also seen stables whose rings are humungus. I don't need a humungus ring, just one that Cactus and I can maneuver in easily.

A third checkpoint is the helpfulness of the other boarders. Boarders who are difficult to get along with can take all the fun out of riding. All of the boarders at my current barn are very helpful and nice and that's the way it ought to be.

My fourth checkpoint is the distance the barn is from my house. I don't want to board at a place that is too far away, or I won't see much of Cactus. If I had my choice, I would keep Cactus in my back yard. The next best thing, though, is a close barn.

My fifth checkpoint involves the vets and farriers. Does the barn owner require you to use a specific vet? Some do. I think that it is better to have your own vet because he will give your horse individualized attention where another one might not.

The same goes for farriers. Maybe your horse needs special shoes and/or has a special problem. If you have your own farrier, he will know exactly what to do.

Barn services are important too. For instance, does the barn owner allow trainers on the premises? Does he provide daily turnout? Some barns don't allow trainers for insurance reasons. Unless you are an accomplished horseman, you'll probably want lessons. Some barns even have different trainers who specialize in different areas of riding.

I also know my horse needs to get out and run, so I insist on a barn that provides daily turnout.

References also have a lot to do with how I choose a barn. For example, if a good friend tells me good things about the barn, I am more likely to give that one a try.

The owner of the barn should play an important role in your barn selection process too. After all, the barn is really a reflection of its owner. He or she is the one who makes the major decisions about the barn and its services. So, a considerate owner is an important ingredient.

Cost is also a major consideration when it comes to choosing a barn. You may spot a barn where you would like to board, and find that it does not fit into your budget. But if you look long and hard enough, you will find one that will make your horse happy and fits into your budget.

My last checkpoint is known as tender loving care (TLC for short). You and I probably give our horses lots of TLC. But when you're not on the premises your horse still needs some TLC from somebody. So make sure you find a loving home for your four-legged friend.

So, if you are in the process of barn hunting, you might want to consider these ten checkpoints. If you cover these bases, your horse will thank you in many different ways. And after all, that is the bottom line, isn't it?

Kiki Osbourne

Happy Cactus

44

How I Got Halfway to my "A"

"Hi, I'm Kiki Osbourne and this my new, 9 year old thoroughbred gelding, Gus. I'm a C-1 member of the St. James Pony Club and today I'd like to try to get my C-2." I introduced myself to my examiner at my C-2 uprating inspection in hopes of having a day of fun and learning ahead of me.

At three o'clock that Sunday morning I had finally crawled into bed for a quick nap before waking up at 6 a.m. to get Gus ready for our rating.

It had been a very busy night. I was cleaning my equipment and, at the same time, I was on the phone with my trainer Kathy Kelly, getting last minute tips on the knowledge part of the rating. She went through all of the requirements and told me exactly how to do everything. After an hour of explaining, I thought I had it all down cold.

I put everything I needed in the car so I would be all ready to leave in the morning. I sat up in bed and thought about what tomorrow would be like.

Six a.m. came quickly and I fell out of bed and into the car, and suddenly I stumbled into the barn to feed Gus breakfast. He'd definitely need his Wheaties today! After I woke up and Gus finished breakfast, I started to spiff him up. Two hours later, he was shiny and ready to be tacked up. I put his saddle and bridle on. Now that Gus looked ready, was I ready? NO.

I ran to the bathroom to change into my breeches, hunt coat and shirt. Boots on, hair up and under my helmet, gloves on, whip in one hand, horse in the other—oh yes, and I almost forgot—my pony club pin! Bill Coaster, "Mr. Examiner," was waiting.

When he finished looking at my tack and asking me about shoeing and feeding, Bill told me to get some warmer clothes on. The three of us "upratees" met in the sand arenas to warm up.

Bill showed up a few minutes later and asked me about the purpose of the different warm-up exercises I did with Gus. I explained that I wanted him to stretch his back and neck, so I worked on a loose rein for a while. I also wanted him to listen to my leg (respond when I put pressure with my legs on the horse's sides) when I asked him to move away from it.

After Gus was all warmed up, we were really ready to work. Bill asked everyone to trot and canter around the arena, in twenty meter circles, and across diagonals. During that time, he gave us suggestions on how to improve our rides. It was kind of like a mini lesson. I like having an examiner who is willing to help rather than one who doesn't say a word throughout the whole test.

After flatwork, we had two more riding tests: Cross Country and stadium jumping.

Our next destination was the "nursery." This is where a lot of smaller Cross Country jumps are enclosed in a pasture. Bill gave us a small course to jump and evaluated our Cross Country skills.

While still in the jumping mode, we decided to finish stadium, too, This time we were allowed to make up a stadium course ourselves. Gus didn't give me any problems, so I was very pleased. Not bad for my first few weeks of riding him.

After jumping, we finally put our horses away while we answered more questions. We had to know about lamenesses, good and bad conformation, nutrition, parasites and disease. At first, I forgot what Kathy told me the night before, but finally I managed to spit it out.

In addition to answering questions, I had to demonstrate how to wrap shipping, standing, and polo bandages. Gus kept his legs still long enough for me to complete one of each. Thank-you, Mr. Gus!

Just when I thought my rating was finished, I was reminded that I had to lunge my horse. Darn! I took Gus out again, put on his "lunging outfit" and put on my lunging equipment. Bill followed us outside where I lunged Gus at the walk, trot, and canter in both directions. He said it was fine and that I was finished — YES!

While the C-1's answered their knowledge questions, I got Gus ready to head home and hoped that I would soon be a C-2.

Bill went into the office for a few minutes to write up several final comments on our requirement sheets. Everyone waited nervously to see the results.

Finally, we were called into the office and...we all passed! I gave a big sigh of relief—it was actually over. Actually, it wasn't as hard as I thought it would be, and now...I'm officially halfway to my "A"!

With my certificate in hand, I led Gus into the trailer and took him home to his nice, cozy stall.

I gave him all the carrots he deserved and promised that our next Pony Club rating would be easier. NOT!

Pony Club Ratings Explained According to the United States Pony Club:

In the USPC, a rating system is used to measure the progress of its members. Standards have been established and are used in all Pony Clubs internationally. Progress is measured in two areas: riding skills and horse management skills. All requirements are detailed in the Pony Club's Standards of Proficiency.

Here are BRIEF, GENERAL explanations of all nine rating levels, as outlined by Pony Club:

The **D1** *Pony Clubber should ride without the lead line, demonstrating basic balance position in an enclosed area at the halt and walk, and control at the walk and trot. The D1 is a beginning level horse manager, willing to learn the simple routines necessary for safe handling of quiet, well trained horses.*

The **D2** *Pony Clubber should ride without the lead line, demonstrating control, while maintaining a safe, basic balanced position at the walk and trot and should begin to develop the canter and jumping position. No need to canter over fences. The candidate should be able to demonstrate simple skills, with assistance if necessary, and should understand the basic reasons for everyday routines of caring for his/her own pony/horse.*

The **D3** *Pony Clubber should ride in a basic balanced position with control at the walk, trot, and canter. He/she should maintain a secure base of support while developing balance and a steady position over fences. The Pony Clubber should be able to demonstrate simple skills of horse management, without assistance, and be able to discuss pony care, using common horse terms.*

The **C1** *Pony Clubber should have confidence and control on the flat and over fences, and demonstrate a basic balanced position and use of natural aids. The rider should begin to initiate free forward movement, and begin to establish light feel of the pony's mouth. The Pony Clubber should show a developing awareness of cause and effect in the care of his/her pony/horse. Assistance is recommended in the demonstration of bandaging.*

The **C2** *Pony Clubber should do all of the above, and show progress toward an independent seat and coordinated use of aids. Free forward movement should be initiated while developing a steady light feel of the pony's mouth. Adding to previous horse management skills, the candidate should be able to bandage, longe, and load, with assistance.*

The **C3** *Pony Clubber adds to the above skills, confidence and control at all gaits on the flat and over fences. The candidate should be competent to care for his/her pony/horse, assuring its comfort and health, while knowing when and where to turn for help if needed. He/she should also be able to explain stable and veterinary routine to D-level Pony Clubbers.*

The **B** *Pony Clubber should also be able to ride each horse forward while establishing and maintaining a regular pace with the horse accepting the aids. He/she should be confident in coping with disobedience. The candidate should be able to explain the application and reasons for aids and to discuss the basic principles of dressage. At this level, the candidate must show sound judgment and maturity in the care of horses and equipment and an understanding of the reasons for what they are doing. He/she must show, through discussion, knowledge of veterinary care, longeing and teaching principles.*

The **H-A** *Pony Clubber must demonstrate a sound knowledge of horses, their care, equipment and training requirements. They must be able to teach stable management and conduct mounted lessons, showing an understanding of safety practices and teaching techniques appropriate to different age levels. He/she must demonstrate the ability to make informed decisions about all aspects of running a barn, including daily routines and emergency procedures*

The **A** *Pony Clubber must be able to ride different horses at various stages of training, and display a confident, consistent, and effective performance on each. He/she must* *demonstrate competence and tact on a school, green, or spoiled horse...discussing or demonstrating schooling techniques required for each horse. Knowledge must be displayed in the proper use of natural and artificial aids.*

Kiki Osbourne

45

An Equispecial Elf

During a 4-H meeting last week, at the home of our 4-H leader, we sat in a room full of green St. Patrick's day decorations. It was so green, I thought a leprechaun was going to jump out of the walls. Little did I know that a few days later at the barn, of all places, my thought would become "reality."

It was late. Everyone had gone home for the night, and I was just hanging up the last cleaned bridle when I heard a voice. I stood very still and, a few seconds later, I heard it again. It said, "I know." *What* did it know? Oh, well, I'm probably just hearing things.

As I walked out of the tack room, hoping I wouldn't hear anything else, I heard a little voice say "I'm here and I know." Finally, I yelled out, "*Who's* here and *what* do you know?" Just then, a shimmering green dust cloud appeared in front of me, and a little green person stood there. (Was he some sort of elf, and should I even talk to this stranger...thinking of my mother's repeated warnings.)

205

"I know what Gus is thinking right now. I communicate with horses."

"You know what Gus is thinking? Yeah. Right, little guy! Go on and just try to get into my horse's head."

"Do you want to know, or should I just get out of here?"

Mmmmmm…an interesting concept, perhaps. "Well I guess I could listen for a second, but make it snappy!"

"Okay. The first thing Gus tells me is that he really likes his new home at Dassenbrook, and he likes the people, too, like Cathy, Kathy, Tiffany, Shannon, Kaitlin and you."

"I kinda figured he liked it here." (So, what's not to like. Good food, good company, bran mash twice a week…he sure has the life!)

"He also wishes that spring was here so the snow would disappear. It would be warmer and he could go outside in the green pastures and eat the delicious green grass. (He'd rather not munch on snow.) He's love to be outside running and playing with another friend like Cactus"

"Wow! This guy's cool!" I thought. "Tell me more," I said. I never knew Gus liked Cactus, the way he squeals at him all the time.

"Let's see. He says he's pretty sure he wants to event this summer. He's not so sure about the Cross Country stuff, but he wants to work on that. He wants to be in the St. James novice event in May, though."

"Good, I was planning on it. Keep going!" (This is VERY helpful. Now I know to work carefully with him on Cross Country.)

"Well, Gosh, what else?" he said scratching his head. "Oh yeah. He'd like a new summer sheet instead of the old ugly, green one he has right now. And, if possible, he wants a new black dressage bridle with white lining because he says he looks good in those."

(Could this be my sub-conscious talking, or my horse? No wonder we get along...we think so much alike!) "I'll have to consult my mom on this one, and I'm sure she won't be happy about it. But, I do plan on getting him a new sheet—so tell him not to worry."

"One last thought before I have to go. Gus said that he really had fun this past weekend at the dressage clinic. The best part was the trailer he got to ride in with his friend, Shade. He said it had tons of room in it, and he didn't feel scrunched. The automatic doors to the indoor arena at St. James Farm scared him, but otherwise, the lesson was fun, and all in all, he enjoyed himself."

"I want to know more...like why he doesn't like me to move the dressage whip from one side to the next, or why does he all of a sudden decide to take a run for no reason and WHY can't I take off my jacket while I'm riding him without him jumping halfway across the arena...THIS inquiring mind wants to know!"

As I was talking the little man started to fade from sight. "Hey, don't go! We've just started the important stuff. Wait…Wait…Well…Thanks a lot, Mr…???"

"Leprechaun," came the very faint reply.

I shook my head, looked up to where he had been, and there was no trace of him. I ran to Gus's stall, half expecting a little man to be perched upon his back. When Gus looked at me, I could swear there was a new twinkle in his eye…or was it just my imagination?

Chester and me

46

Free Horses?

Anyone want a free horse? Well, there is a way to get a very good horse for FREE...and I'm here to tell you about it. You say there's no such thing as a "free" horse? Well, actually, you're only half right!

LEASING. That's the keyword. With a lease, you don't actually buy the horse. Rather you pay for the general maintenance of the horse. It is like "borrowing" a horse, but not having to pay thousands of dollars right up front.

There are many horse owners who are willing make this arrangement. If you are trying to convince your parents to take that BIG step into horse ownership, this may be a way to ease into it. It will certainly tell you if you really are ready for this big responsibility, without a huge financial investment. And, if things don't work out, you are not left with a horse to sell.

There are many different types of leases you could look into. One is a half lease. This means that you generally agree to pay half the horse's board bill. In some cases you may also split vet and farrier bills.

Not only do you split upkeep costs, but you must also split riding time. Usually each person gets to ride and take care of the horse for 3 days, and the seventh day is a rest day. I've found that it's best to have a pre-arranged schedule of when each person rides — that way there's no confusion. A calendar on the horse's stall usually works well to keep a daily record of ride times. If someone rides, they record what they did that day.

You must also have your own equipment. This means grooming tools and tack. Many owners may be willing to share grooming tools, but tack is another story. This will probably be the biggest investment you will have to make, outside of actually purchasing the horse. Which you are not doing, at this point, remember! Once you have your own tack, though, you will be able to use it when you are ready to move on to buying your own horse.

If you'd rather have this "free horse" all to yourself, another option is a full lease. In this case, you pay for all of the expenses for the normal upkeep of the horse. In most full leases, the horse is "yours" as long as you are paying. Again, though, this is an agreement reached by the owner and the lessee.

In most lease agreements I have seen, there is no money paid initially for the horse. Therein lies the difference between buying and leasing. However, there are some instances where there is a lease fee involved as well. This generally happens with very "high ticket" horses. Most of the people I know who are involved with leasing do not have pay anything other than upkeep of the horse.

The lessee is simply totally responsible for the maintenance of the horse, according to a signed lease agreement, which may list many "terms." Some of these terms include the amount and type of riding that may be done with the horse. It may also include places that the horse may or may not travel to and certain dates that he cannot be used.

Leasing also can be a big advantage to the person who owns the horse. If someone has a horse that they refuse to sell, but can't afford the monthly board payments, a lease would work out great.

For example, I would never want to sell my first horse, Cactus, because I love him so much. But I have to move on to another horse…and I could never afford to keep TWO horses. So, we asked several people we knew if they would be interested in leasing my good friend.

I was very lucky to find a family who wanted to lease Cactus. They love him, take care of him, and ride him just the way I had been riding him in Pony Club. This is also very good for Cactus, who was beginning to be a "one woman" horse. Fortunately, I have another advantage in that he is kept only one stall away from my new horse, so I get to see him all the time.

I've looked into leasing horses and found that there are many advantages to doing so. First, leasing always gives you first-hand experience of what owning a horse is really like. Second, there is more of a chance to ride a good, experienced horse that you might otherwise not be able to afford. Last, the initial expenses for leasing the horse won't be nearly as expensive as owning your own.

Where can you find a "free" horse? You can start by asking local barn managers if there is anyone who is looking to lease a horse. A good source is a local equine publication, or your local newspapers. Tack shops have bulletin boards that advertise horses for sale as well. You might even try to call people who are selling their horses. They may be willing to lease, if they can't find a buyer immediately. You might even work out a lease with an option to buy, if you get along well with the horse.

You CAN have a new horse this show season. Be resourceful, start looking, and it will happen. A free horse? YES!

47

Tackling Your Tack

Since I joined Pony Club, I've learned a lot about clean and safe tack. I never understood why it was important until one of my instructors ripped apart the stitching of my stirrup leathers. I was shocked to see how easily it ripped. Now that it's winter and we don't ride as much, it's a perfect time to do some nit-picky tack checks.

The first step in checking your tack is cleaning it up. Expect to get dirty when you do this. If you stay clean, you must be doing something wrong!

Pony Club suggests that we clean our tack using warm water and glycerine soap. Use a natural sponge to soap up EVERY area of your saddle. The easiest way to clean a bridle thoroughly is to take it apart. (Just make sure you know how to put it back together!) In hard to reach places, like around buckles, a toothbrush or a toothpick works great.

When my tack is clean, I look over the stitching on the stirrup leathers first. I pull as hard as I can on the stitched leather. If the stitching rips, it's time to get the leathers re-stitched, or to buy a new pair. Another thing I check is the wear of the leather where the stirrup hangs. After a year or two, the leather stretches, gets thin and runs the risk of breaking while you ride. You can imagine a rider, riding Cross Country, a stirrup leather rips, the stirrup falls off, the horse spooks, the rider loses his/her balance, and risks injury, just because he/she did not routinely check the tack.

The billets (the part of the saddle where you attach your girth) are another essential part of the saddle that should be checked. If you don't believe your billets should be checked, think of it this way: They are your lifeline. If they rip, the saddle falls off. The stitching usually lasts longer here than anywhere else on the saddle, but it should always be routinely checked with the other equipment.

Stitching on the girth (the part of the saddle that goes under the belly of the horse, holding the saddle in place) is also important. The girth, too, is your lifeline. A few times I've gone out to ride, put the girth on, and noticed it ripping apart. I didn't ride because I didn't feel very safe using a girth with rotted stitching.

Your bridle is also critical. It holds the bit which gives you control of the horse. I think the reins are the most important. If a rein breaks you have no control or at least only half control!

Every place that is stitched is critical and should be checked. Take the time now during these cold winter days to check every inch of leather you and your horse use. Then, promise yourself that you will regularly clean, check, and repair or replace your tack.

NOW, get ready to enjoy a new, fun, SAFE show season. See ya there!

Kiki Osbourne

Eventing with Gus

Stadium

48

My First Official USCTA Event

During Spring break, my mom and I ran all over Florida looking for a mailbox that would postmark my important entry form for the USCTA St. James event...my FIRST official USCTA event with my new horse. Finally, late that night, we found a post office that stamped March 30 on it.

I spent over an hour filling out that entry form for this event. I checked and re-checked to make sure everything was just perfect. Everything was signed, my USCTA number was on the form, the division was right, and the stabling form was filled out. I even made one last long distance phone call from Florida to my trainer to double check! On an official USCTA entry form, everything had to be just right or else they'd say, "Sorry Charlie." I wouldn't want to miss this event.

A few weeks after I frantically mailed the entry, I received a letter from St. James Farm. I ripped it open right away. It said I was accepted as a Junior Novice rider and Gus would be stabled at Danada equestrian

Center down the road. Cool! I was so excited—I was officially in the event! What I failed to realize at the time was that we would have to tie our horses to our trailer at the actual event...and Gus had never been tied to a trailer before.

Only the first hurdle had been jumped. Now I had to prepare myself and Gus to compete. Lately, the weather had not been cooperating, so I still needed to take Gus outside for the first time this year. Little did I know what a job it would be to keep him calm. For a few days he was sure the Gus eating monster was out to get him.

Since I had the St. James event in mind all winter, I did tons of dressage and took lots of flat lessons so I could put in a good dressage test. Most of the time we did all right. I had a Cross Country lesson and many Stadium Jumping lessons before the big week-end. I was prepared (so I thought).

The week-end before we left for St. James we rode at a hunter show in a three-foot jumping class especially made for us to practice stadium jumping before the event. I fell off twice in schooling and my rounds didn't deserve a ribbon, so I got a little worried about the next week-end.

Finally, the day arrived when we trailered to Danada. Since my mother FORCED me to go to school that first day, my trainer had to trailer Gus. I met him there after school to make sure he settled in. He seemed happy to be stabled next to his partner in crime, Shade Dancer.

After seeing Gus, I drove to St. James Farm to go on the official novice Cross Country course walk with my trainer Cathy Jones, Kathy Corkran, Kathy Kelly, and Liz. Did you ever notice how popular the name "Kathy" is in the equestrian world? Anyway, I remembered the course from last fall when I rode it for a "Fun Day." I couldn't wait to ride it again.

On our way out the door to get back to ride the horses at Danada we grabbed some pop and pizza...a little treat for all competitors of the event who attended the course walk. Hey! This eventing is okay!

The first thing we did at Danada was pack the trailer so we could leave early Saturday morning. I am very lucky to have Shade Dancer's owner as a good friend, because Shade has become Gus'ss best friend as well, and we can trailer together to these events. I then took Gus out for a short hack (a light, easy workout) to relax him (and me?) a bit.

Since we were trailering together, Liz spent the week-end with us. We went home to get some sleep before the BIG day.

My alarm rang at 4:30 a.m. and we flew out of bed to put more things in my van. Within 15 minutes we were on our way to Danada to braid Gus and Shade's manes. They had to look stunning for Dressage.

I was scheduled to ride my dressage test at 8:36 (approximately!) a.m. By then, I was calming down. Luckily, I had two friends helping me brush and tack up Gus while I got dressed.

Finally I was on and went to warm up as usual. Gus thought there were monsters chasing him — so the warm-up didn't go as well as planned. The test was not great. Gus only "lost it" twice. I was disappointed with our performance, as Gus's specialty had been Dressage. I told myself that this was just the first event of the season, and we just need to get in the groove.

Gus spent the afternoon resting, like me, and of course thinking about stadium (or at least I did!) Soon I was warming up for jumping. He seemed "brave" today and jumped everything except fence #2. I was pleased with our performance. By the end of the day we were in 14th place out of 21 riders. Not bad for our first event...it was that dressage score and fence #2 that did not help us at all that day.

Sunday was going to be a good Cross Country day...I could feel it. Gus was as ready to go as I was. We walked the course earlier, so I knew where I was going, but would Gus?

Gus and Shade were relaxing back at Danada when we went to pick them up. (They must have known and saved their energy!) After we unloaded them at St. James, they got studs put in their back shoes so they would have more traction when they jumped. (Studs are like the spikes that baseball players use.)

Finally, after putting on all Gus's and my Cross Country stuff (studs, splint boots, jumping vest, helmet, crop) we were ready. Gus was really cool about the warm-up thing—I wish he would have been this quiet in dressage warm-up! Anyway, we jumped a few fences and the starters called for us. Gus and I walked to the starting box, they counted down and said that magic word: GO!

We cantered out of the box, and over fence #1. Now was the fun part. I talked to Gus the whole way as we galloped over the rest of the fences in that wonderful picturesque course to the finish. Gus took every fence in stride and had no problems at all. I was soooo excited! My first clean Cross Country round! At the finish I got off and walked him for a LONG time. I told him how good he was and that he deserved LOTS of carrots. He took me up on the offer.

They announced the scores as we were poulticing and wrapping our horses. Liz and I weren't in the ribbons, but it didn't matter. We had a wonderful "event"ful week-end. By the way, we learned a lot about eventing at this competition, not the least of which was that Gus WILL tie to a trailer if he is with his friend, Shade. THAT'S progress! Now it's on to the Wayne for the Horse Trials in June. WE "R" EVENTING!

Author's Note:

The USCTA has recently changed its name to USEA (United States Eventing Association).

Horse Trials/Events include three phases: Dressage, Cross Country and Show Jumping. Each level has increasing degrees of difficulty. These are described in the USA Equestrian Rules for Eventing. Briefly, these levels are:

Beginner Novice. Designed to introduce green (Inexperienced) horses and riders to the sport. It should be safe, inviting and educational, to build confidence and a desire to continue. Jumps will be a maximum of 2'9".

Novice. The dressage test will include walk, trot, canter with 20 meter figures, and a halt. Jumping is intended to be a positive experience, with a maximum height of 2'11".

Training. Intended for competitors and horses with some experience and training. The jumping courses may have two or more elements per jump, and a maximum height of 3'3".

Preliminary. The cross country jumps require accuracy, agility, boldness, control, judgment and jumping ability. The Stadium jumps will emphasize quickness or recovery and may require lengthening or shortening stride. Maximum height for this level is 3"7".

Intermediate. More technical difficulty is added at this level. Expect to see banks, ditches, water, and narrow jumps. Maximum height is 3'9".

Advanced. This is the highest national level of Horse trials. Dressage may include extensions at all gaits, and single flying lead changes. Maximum height is 3'11". Jumps increase in technical difficulty, and the widths of the jumps are increased as well.

To learn more about Eventing, go to their website at www.eventingusa.com.

49

An Equispecial End to Area IV's Event Season

The week-end of October 9th and 10th seemed like the middle of winter. Officials, judges and competitors alike walked around all bundled up. Many said that this should be renamed the Evergreen Farm "Winter" Horse Trials. But, the weather was the least of our concerns, as we knew the season's last Horse Trials in Area IV must go on.

Friday, after the unloading frenzy was over and most of the horses were settled in their stalls for the weekend, the riders prepared themselves for the official Cross Country course walk. About 135 competitors put on layers of clothing and grabbed a cup of hot, steamy coffee and course maps to wait for the TD (technical delegate) to arrive.

Novice and training riders separated to look over their own courses. Twenty minutes later, after finishing their walks, small clumps of frozen people started to come back into the barn to get warm, feed their horses, and say good night. Around nine o'clock, when our group finally left, we switched off the lights and all was quiet at the farm — until the next day.

At five-thirty Saturday morning it was still quiet, but the lights were on, and everyone was working (some with half-opened eyes) braiding and grooming their mounts for the day ahead. As the sun came up, the riders came to life, putting on their formal dress and warming up their mounts.

The training championship division led off the dressage tests, followed by open training and, finally, novice. Through the morning mist we could see the warm-up arena filled with horses and riders with winter coats over their riding coats. It made me cold just watching them. Around noon, one ring was taken down, which made Dressage fall slightly behind schedule. This turned out to be a challenge for the junior novice riders, as their Cross Country rides would be coming up quicker.

The training division was done with their Cross Country rides well before novice finished Dressage. So, Cross Country now ran ahead of schedule, and it kept getting more and more ahead. The Junior novice riders had only an hour or so to pull out braids, put on boots, change tack and change clothes. Before we knew it, the juniors were in the Cross Country warm-up and headed to the start. Nothing seemed to matter except to ride the course as we had planned during our course walk.

The weather really was a factor at this event. It rained on Saturday morning. That, combined with the cold and the wind, made for a very uncomfortable feeling for the riders. The Cross Country course was soft and slippery in spots, and I believe that both riders and their mounts were trying to be cautious and safe.

After the long, cold day of Dressage and Cross Country, we poulticed and wrapped all the horses. Everyone was beat, so they fed their horses as soon as they could and headed back to hotels to get some sleep for stadium day at the Evergreen horse trials. I think both riders and horses slept well dreaming about that gorgeous stadium round they would have Sunday (and that the weather would be better!).

The training championship riders began their stadium rounds at about 8:30 a.m. in the sunshine (our dreams did come true!). At the end of the division, the results were figured, and the Training Championship winner was announced. Then, the optimum time was adjusted slightly, making it slower in the open training divisions.

The course was lowered, and the triple line was taken down when the fences were adjusted to novice height. A small amount of time was allowed for the novice riders to walk the course, and the novice divisions began.

Competitors started to pack up as soon as their group finished and, by the time the juniors were done, there were only a few people left to load horses and say good-bye to Evergreen for the winter.

Ego and me

50

Pony Club Rally on my First "Catch Ride"

What a pleasant surprise. I step off the plane after a three-week vacation, and the first thing I hear from my friend Liz is that my horse Gus is lame. I thought she was joking until my mother confirmed Liz's report, so I knew it was true.

Okay, I can deal with this. I have spent three weeks away from my favorite four-legged friend, can't wait to ride again, and have the Pony Club Regional Combined Training Rally coming up in three days. Great.

I had already decided that the barn would be my first stop after depositing the luggage at home. Now I wanted to get there as fast as I could.

When I finally arrived at the barn, I saw that my friend Gus was just a bit "off" and would probably not be ready in three days for a combined training competition. The vet confirmed this suspicion. I couldn't ride Gus this year at that rally, and my only

229

alternative was my good old buddy Cactus. However, he was a bit out of shape and I didn't want to risk his well-being.

Then came the offer. My trainer Cathy Jones, told me that my friend Tiffany had offered "Ego," her second horse, to me. I made my decision to ride him in a minute. I WAS going to ride in that rally. I had never ridden anyone else's horse in a serious competition, but I was ready to take the challenge.

Little did I know what I would encounter. How would I actually feel riding a different horse, especially one I'd never ridden?

I couldn't waste time. That afternoon I had a flat lesson on Ego. I actually felt confident riding him. This may not be so bad after all!

Ego was a totally different horse from my Gus. I had to ride him with hardly any contact on his mouth, whereas Gus requires more contact. Throughout the whole lesson he was consistent and in control, the most I could ask for in a first ride.

The next day we were scheduled to leave for the rally, so I decided to have a jumping lesson on Ego. This was a good decision, because I'd have to jump in two of the three phases. I have to admit, I was nervous after hearing all of the "Ego jumping" stories from those who knew and loved him. After I jumped a few successful fences, we packed up and headed out with Ego in the trailer.

As soon as I arrived at the rally, kids kept asking, "Who's your horse?" Then they asked me, "Why in the world would you set foot on Ego?" I guess most of them were at the C rally last year where he put in a wild performance around the Cross Country course and stadium.

Everyone wished me luck, but they said it as if the word "luck" had two syllables: "Good lu-uck." I began to wonder...but, I was determined to prove everyone wrong. We WOULD jump everything clean and get a decent dressage score, I told myself.

When you're riding someone else's horse, it is not just the riding that you have to be concerned with, but also his overall well-being. I worried about leaving him overnight—what if he were hurt during the night? But the next morning he was standing in his stall, waiting to eat.

I know for sure that he got the royal treatment. Before my formal inspection, we shined up Ego, polished his feet, and wiped his face with baby oil. WOW! What a horse! The judge at formals said he was very, very clean, and I was told "good luck" riding him. (There was that phrase again!)

I was so excited in the Dressage warm-up because he was going very nicely! I found the more I rode him, the better he got. Hopefully, he'd be just like that during my test. I didn't have much time to get to know Ego, but I'm sure we bonded in that half hour before we headed to the dressage arena. (HA!)

Finally, I was told to go into the arena. Ego scared himself when he saw his reflection in the water puddles. Good start. But, overall, I was happy with our score because I was a bit nervous myself.

After Dressage, it was one day down, one to go. Tomorrow would be the real challenge: Cross Country

AND stadium. I could hear all of those "good lu-ucks" now!

We were up early to prepare. I walked the Cross Country course once more and went back to get Ego ready.

I put boots, saddle and bridle on Ego, and got myself ready. After a safety check, I warmed up, and coach Cathy Jones helped us jump. Thank heavens Cathy was there, because she trains and rides Ego and knows him better than I. After a hard warm-up we headed for the Cross Country start.

I tried to remember everything I'd been told. He'll probably look at everything. Go slow! Keep your leg on him! Just kick to the fence! Ride aggressively!

"Five, four, three, two, one, GO!" We cantered out of the starting box, looked at the first fence and popped over. From there on it was smooth sailing. We galloped (really fast) around the course and jumped everything. No time penalties here! We dashed through the finish, out of breath. I hardly ever work THAT hard when I ride Gus.

Tiffany said we looked good, but it felt too FAST. Oh well, we went clean, which was all I asked for. Maybe those good luck wishes paid off!

Before I could catch my breath, we were walking the stadium course, and I was warming up again for yet another round of jumping. By this time Ego and I were really a team. After all, we had been working together for several days now. And I DID remember to give him carrots after our Cross Country ride.

So we went in the arenas and braved the jumps for another clean round. Well, maybe I hadn't ridden the best ride, but it was clean—again, that's what I asked. Thanks to Tiffany, thanks to Cathy Jones, thanks to Ego, thanks to all my friends wishing my good lu-uck, my experience on a new mount proved to be successful.

I figured all in all it was really a good experience for me. The moral of this story? If you want to be a rider, you have to be flexible. In the horse world, you never know what waits around the next bend. So, be prepared. In fact, be EQUISPECIALLY prepared!

Oh, the fun I had*! (Clockwise from lower left: Cactus, Brittany, Gene, Outryder, Gus, Chester)*

51

An Equispecial Good-Bye

Okay, I've got to face it. It's time for me to grow up. But writing my Equispecial Kids Column for the past five years has been a wonderful experience. I've learned so much about the horse world by researching my stories. I've met so many people I'd never have met without my writing. So now, since a new kid's columnist will be taking the reins next month, I'd like to take this opportunity to thank a bunch of people who have been an important part of the past five Equispecial years.

First, I'd like to thank Felicitas (Fel) Camacho for taking a chance on a kid with no professional writing experience. As some of you may know, five years ago my father and I both submitted articles to Fel at the same time. Mine was a short paper on grooming and general care for horses. My dad's was on exercise for riders. I didn't really expect anyone to seriously consider mine. But not only did Fel consider it, she liked it and published it! That put me on the road to an Equispecial writing experience with the Equine Market.

I want to thank my parents for encouraging me to write regularly. Every month they hounded me, making sure I made my deadlines. Most of my pieces still get a little editing from Mom or Dad and they never let me get away with writing sloppy stuff.

It's not easy to come up with material on my own month after month. So, most of the time, I've asked others for their opinions on various horse-related subjects. I want to thank all of you who have given me your ideas and opinions over the past five years.

For example, to all the interviewees featured in my stories, I want to say thanks. These include at least, Liz Rice (saddleseat rider), Terese Soloman (Dressage trainer), Marcie Young (and her horse, Magnetic), John Davies (from St. James Farm) and Kathy Kelly (Back to Basics). Other friends and acquaintances who have helped me in various ways are Jim Pehta, Torey Thornbrugh, Liz Mueller, the Joy family and my fellow pony clubbers.

All the horses mentioned in my column deserve an Equispecial thanks. They all did something outstanding to get my attention. Whether it was Cactus going to my first event with me, Magnetic taking me through the hunter shows, Ego being there when I needed a horse for C rally, Brittany, my first mount, Outryder, Gene, or Gus. I love you all!

A column is pointless, though, without an audience who reads it. So thanks to all of you who have read my column month in and month out and enjoyed it. Some of you even wrote letters to express your own opinions and it always made me feel super when you took the time and effort to respond.

Finally, I'd like to thank Kandee Haertel for encouraging me to switch from the Equispecial Kids Column to an Equispecial adult's commentary. Yes, Equispecial will still be around, you see. But the audience will be a little different, a little older. But we're all still kids at heart, right? Tally ho, for now!

Dappir and me

Slim Chance and me

Epilogue

It's been many years since I wrote that last good-bye column. As I said, life goes on and we grow up, no matter what. Aside from my growing older, many things have changed since then. Let's see...

I did achieve my Pony Club A rating in 1996. That led me to a job as a trainer/instructor at Hunter Oaks Farm in Carlock Illinois. When I got my horse, Dappir, from Virginia, it hooked me up with Shenandoah Farm, where I was offered a position as barn manager & trainer. So, off I went to spend four wonderful years in the Shenandoah Valley, teaching, training and competing. Lured back to the Midwest by Hunter Oaks Farm, I remain there today as the head instructor/trainer.

You may be wondering...whatever happened to some of the people, places and horses in the book? I still keep in contact with all the "Kathys." Kathy Kelly, PhD, is in Ocala Florida. Cathy Jones-Forsburg rides and trains out of Topline Equestrian Center in Hampshire, IL.

The Joy's Farm, Kingsway, is now also home to the Friends for Therapeutic Equine Activities.

And those horses...Brittany lived a good life with a wonderful woman who was her best friend, until Brit fractured her leg, and had to be humanely destroyed. Gene's Big Dream is living at Virginia Tech, enjoying stardom in their riding program. After his wildly successful racing career, Zip Plus Four became an event horse who now lives with his great owner, Mary Francis, in Champaign, Ilinois. Outryder lived a blissful life with a Pony Club family, in Illinois, until she also had to be humanely destroyed after a chronic illness. Magic Ryder fractured her leg while winning a race, but was able to spend the rest of her life as a broodmare with my friend, Heidi Henry. Gus is having a good time with a new friend, competing in local horse trials. And Cactus, my main man, lived a pampered life with my friends Sharon and Jill Westerholm, until age 26, when he went peacefully to that great pasture in the sky.

And the horses I have now...they have been wonderful teachers just like their friends before them. Chester is a 25 year old thoroughbred who I rode at many training and preliminary events. He now helps me teach lessons. Slim Chance, a 17 year old thoroughbred, took me to my first three day event where we finished successfully in 17th place. Dappir...and I can't say enough about this 17 year old Akhal Teke-Thoroughbred...he took me to my "A" and beyond. He took me to my first preliminary, and later, my first Intermediate event, and won it!

As for the future...I am always looking ahead for the next challenge. I am looking forward to competing and meeting many more horses in my lifetime. And I am sure that they will all hold special places in my heart as those before them. I plan to continue competing, and following my dream of participating in international competition. And when that happens, maybe I'll be ready to sit down and write another book.

Acknowledgments

I would like to thank my parents for believing in my dreams and helping support my horse life, and for encouraging me to put pen to paper so that I now have a recorded history of my life as a young rider. I appreciate all the work they did to put the finishing touches on this book. Thanks to my brother Cody for spending hours scanning photos and artwork for the initial editing phases. He also helped design the cover of this book. My Grandma and Grandpa Skwira were always ready to help, and made the time to come and watch me ride, and offer encouragement, even in some really rotten weather! And Grandma and Grandpa Osbourne always cheered me from afar back in Iowa.

I had the good fortune to work with some of the best trainers in the area. I started with Heidi Henry, who took the time to teach me the basics of horse care after we bought our first horse, and she introduced me to huntseat and jumping. As I moved on, I continued to be surrounded by good people. Kathy Kelly was always there with support and enthusiasm for my riding, horse career, and now this book. Cathy Jones-Forsburg has been there as a coach, special friend, has helped me get to where I am today, and continues to do so. Thanks to the two major (K)Cathy's in my life.

And then there are my mom's friends! Out of the goodness of their hearts, they gave their time to help with the book. Roseanne Soulides helped input all the articles into the computer, when we found that all of the articles were stored on our OLD computer, which we don't have anymore! Jari Lynn Franklin and Colette Verdun added lots of editing expertise. Susan ("Sue") Leston not only contributed her editing expertise, but saved the day by offering her graphics skills in the final composition phase of the book. The Dotto family, Bob, Kathy, John, and Sarah lent their computer power to my Mom in the final hour. And then, Dulcey Lima showed extreme patience working through the final CD ROM glitches. Thanks, Mom's friends.

Special thanks goes to all my horses, past and present. In particular, I thank Phil and Margot Case for giving me the opportunity to ride the BEST horse in the whole world, Dappir...and many of his half siblings. And also their horses, Kandu, Kurina, and Goldka. Thanks again to Cathy for letting me ride/compete "Chet" (Chester). I wouldn't be here if it weren't for all of my other four legged friends: Brittany, Cactus, Outryder, Gene, Gus, and Slim.

I have had an opportunity to cultivate some wonderful friendships in the horse world. So, I say thanks to all of my friends who made the journey with me in this book, and to my students and clients, both in Illinois & Virginia. I couldn't have done it then, and I couldn't do it now, without you!

Last but not least, I must not leave out the small but mighty Baily and Britches, my two Jack Russell Terriers, who sit patiently waiting for me day after day, and always manage to make me smile after a long day at the barn. They watched as I put the finishing touches on this book and only tried to tap the keyboard once or twice. Good dogs.

Good dogs, Baily and Britches

My brother Cody and me on Cactus and Brittany…where it all began…

About the Author

Kiki Osbourne is the trainer/instructor with Dappir Ridge Eventing in Charlottesville, VA. She is a combined training competitor, a graduate "A" of Pony Club, a member of the USEA (United States Eventing Association), USA Equestrian, and The American Horse Trials Foundation. As a young rider (ages 12-16) "learning the ropes" by taking lessons, being an active member of Pony Club and 4H, she wrote a monthly column called *Equispecial, A Horse Column for Kids*, in order to help support her four legged friend named Cactus. She has put together 51 of her best *Equispecial* columns with some of her artwork (done during the same time period) and brought them together into a very special book.

www.ingramcontent.com/pod-product-compliance
Lightning Source LLC
Chambersburg PA
CBHW031244090426
42742CB00007B/306